Speak the Blessing

Send Your Words
in the Direction You Want
Your Life to Go

JOEL OSTEEN

Nashville   New York

Also by Joel Osteen

Speak the
Blessing

FaithWords
Hachette Book Group
1290 Avenue of the Americas, New York, NY 10104
faithwords.com
X.com/faithwords

First Edition: April 2024

FaithWords is a division of Hachette Book Group, Inc. The FaithWords
name and logo are trademarks of Hachette Book Group, Inc.

The publisher is not responsible for websites (or their content) that are not
owned by the publisher.

The Hachette Speakers Bureau provides a wide range of authors for
speaking events. To find out more, go to hachettespeakersbureau.com or
email HachetteSpeakers@hbgusa.com.

FaithWords books may be purchased in bulk for business, educational,
or promotional use. For information, please contact your local
bookseller or the Hachette Book Group Special Markets Department
at special.markets@hbgusa.com.

Library of Congress Cataloging-in-Publication Data
Names: Osteen, Joel, author.
Title: Speak the blessing : send your words in the direction you want your life
to go / Joel Osteen.
Description: First edition. | Nashville : FaithWords, 2024.
Identifiers: LCCN 2023041041 | ISBN 9781546005117 (hardcover) | ISBN
9781546006817 (large print) | ISBN 9781546005131 (ebook)
Subjects: LCSH: Conversation—Religious aspects—Christianity. |
Interpersonal communication—Religious aspects—Christianity. | Praise—
Religious aspects—Christianity. | Self-talk—Religious aspects—Christianity.
Classification: LCC BV4597.53.C64 O88 2024 | DDC
241/.672—dc23/eng/20231010
LC record available at https://lccn.loc.gov/2023041041

ISBN: 9781546005117 (hardcover), 9781546006817 (large print),
9781546005131 (ebook)

Printed in Canada.

LSC

MQR. Printing 1, 2024

Contents

Introduction

At the beginning of our Lakewood services, we repeat a list of "I Am" declarations that starts with "I am blessed." The Scripture says, "He who invokes a blessing on himself shall do so by saying, 'May the God of truth bless me.'" The way you bless yourself is to say what God says about you. "I am strong. I am talented. I am forgiven. I am healthy. I am valuable. I am a masterpiece." Those are not just positive affirmations; you just invoked a blessing on yourself. When you speak it out, you give life to what you're saying. When you say, "I am blessed," blessings come looking for you. When you say, "I am prosperous," good breaks start tracking you down.

Your words have the power to change your life, and that's why I've written this book. I want to help you know how to declare faith-filled words that invite blessings and favor into your life. You can start to enjoy a life filled with freedom, confidence, joy, and creativity by discovering the power of speaking God's Word. When you dare to believe and speak the blessings and promises He has given, when you send your words out in the direction you want your life to go, they will put you on a path to better health, abundance, success, and new levels of your destiny. You will discover unique abilities and advantages you never knew you had. And best of all, you will become the amazing masterpiece that you were created to be.

When you speak the blessing, it can work wonders. The life-changing possibilities are unlimited.

CHAPTER ONE

Miracles in Your Mouth

Get your heart and your words going
in the right direction and just dare to
say what God says about you.

Our words have creative power. When we speak something out, we're giving it the right to come to pass. It's one thing to believe you're healed, but when you say "I am healed," that's what releases the healing. It's not enough to just believe you have favor, believe that you're blessed, believe that you're going to fulfill your dreams. The Scripture says that the spirit of faith is in your words. When you say, "I am blessed. I have favor. I am coming out of debt," angels go to work, good breaks will find you, and the right people will track you down. You can think positively, you can believe that you will receive favor, you can pray for God's blessings, and that's all good. But nothing happens until you speak the blessing. The miracle is in your mouth. There is healing in your mouth, there is freedom in your mouth, and there are new levels in your mouth.

If you're fighting a sickness, it's easy to talk about the medical report and how bad it looks. "I don't think I'll ever get well."

> *Nothing happens until you speak the blessing.*

When you speak that out, you're calling in more defeat, more sickness. You need to change what you're saying. The Scripture says, "Let the weak say, 'I am strong.'" It doesn't say, "Let the weak talk about the weakness. Let the weak call five friends and discuss the problem." That's giving life to the negative. I'm not asking you to deny the facts of the sickness, but just say what God says about you. Your report should be: "God is restoring health to me. He will fulfill the number of my days."

My mother wouldn't be alive today, after being diagnosed with terminal liver cancer in 1981, if she had not done this. It's not enough to just not say anything negative about it. That's good, but you have to be on the offensive. All through the day I would hear her quoting scriptures. When someone asked how she was doing, it was never a sad song. "Poor old me. It's hard. I don't understand it." Her report was: "I am healed. With long life, God will satisfy me. What He started in my life, He's going to finish." She didn't feel healed, and her circumstances didn't look any different. She felt weak, but she said, "I am strong." The medical report said she was done, but she said, "I will live and not die." She got in agreement with God and released the miracle in her mouth. Forty-three years later, she's still alive and healthy.

Are there miracles in your mouth waiting to be released? "Joel, when I get free from this addiction, I'll tell people I'm free." You have to tell them first. You need to declare every day, "I am free. I am clean. This addiction doesn't control me." You may say, "That's not telling the truth." No, that's the weak saying, "I am strong." You have to release the miracle. When you say, "I am free," chains are broken in the unseen realm, strongholds are loosed. Freedom starts heading your way. You keep speaking it, and you will become what you're saying. You are prophesying your future. Listen to the words coming out of your mouth.

> *Are there miracles in your mouth waiting to be released?*

SPEAK TO YOUR GIANT

When David faced Goliath, a giant twice his size, it wasn't a coincidence that David looked at him and said, "This day I will strike you down and cut off your head." He wasn't just being positive, and he wasn't just talking smack. He understood this principle that the miracle was in his mouth. He had to release the victory. What would have happened if David had said, "Wow! I thought I wanted to fight him, but look how big he is. I don't have any armor, and I don't feel qualified. I don't have a chance"? If he had talked defeat, we wouldn't know who David was. If he had just thought positively, *I can do this. I know I have what it takes*, he wouldn't have defeated Goliath. David knew the miracle was in his mouth, so he spoke it out. "I will defeat you." You may have a giant in your path, a giant of debt, a giant of sickness, a giant of depression. You need to announce to that giant: "I will defeat you. You are not going to keep me from my destiny. The forces for me are greater than the forces trying to stop me."

The Scripture says, "If two of you agree about anything you ask for according to God's will, it will be done for them." There's power in agreement. What's interesting is that David didn't have anyone to agree with him. His brothers looked down on him and thought he was too small. His father saw him as less-than and didn't bring him into the house when the prophet Samuel was choosing one of his sons as the next king of Israel. King Saul didn't think David had a chance. He tried to give David his armor to at least make it a little less painful. Nobody was there to encourage him and say, "David, you can do this. We're behind you. We know you have what it takes." As with David, there are times when you can't find anyone to agree with you. But I've learned that there is power when you come into agreement with yourself, when you get your heart and mouth in agreement and start speaking the blessing, start declaring that you are well able, that you have the victory, that you will defeat an addiction. Then even if others don't agree with you, because you're in agreement with yourself, you will see giants defeated

> *There is power when you come into agreement with yourself, when you get your heart and mouth in agreement and start speaking the blessing.*

and accomplish dreams that others thought were impossible.

Quit being discouraged because nobody is cheering you on and nobody sees what you see. Sometimes God puts things in your heart that others can't understand. It seems too big and impossible. Instead of encouraging you, they do just the opposite. "You think you can defeat that cancer. I don't know. Your grandmother died of the same thing." "After all these years, you still think you're going to have a baby. You're kind of getting up there in years." "Do you really think you're going to start an orphanage, or write a book, or lead your department, or move into a nice neighborhood? I just don't see it." The good news

> *You have to say it before you'll see it.*

is, they don't have to see it. You don't need them to agree with you. Come into agreement with yourself. Get your heart and words going in the right direction. Start talking like it's going to happen. You have to say it before you'll see it.

DARE TO DECLARE WHAT GOD PUT
IN YOUR HEART

When David went out to face Goliath, all the soldiers in the Israeli and the Philistine armies were watching. All they saw was a small teenager who looked like a boy, with no military training, no experience, and no armor. Yet in front of them all, David had the audacity to say with confidence, "Goliath, I will defeat you." Some of the soldiers ridiculed and made fun of him. The Scripture says that Goliath looked on David with contempt and said, "Am I a dog that you come at me with sticks, sending this little boy? Is this all you've got?" Sometimes people around you won't see the greatness in you. They'll judge you by the outside, by your size, your background, your experience, your nationality. Don't let them talk you out of what God put in your heart. They don't have to agree with you. Do as David did and speak the victory in spite of what the naysayers think. Declare your vision in spite of what the experts are telling you. People don't determine your destiny. They don't know what God put in you. Don't let their negative words keep you from speaking positive, faith-filled words.

When we were trying to acquire the former Compaq Center for our church facility, it was like David versus Goliath. The company that we were up against was the largest taxpayer in Texas, a huge real estate company. There were a lot of people who didn't think we had a chance. It wasn't just the critics, but even some of the experts. Deep down I knew God put this in my heart. I knew it wasn't enough to just believe that it was going to happen. Faith is released when we speak it out. So I announced to the congregation that we were going to purchase the Compaq Center. Over the next three years, there was all kinds of opposition and many times when it looked as though it would never work out. I was tempted to talk about what I saw. "Our opponents are so strong. They have more funds and influence. I don't see how it's going to happen." But I understood this principle: We give life to whatever we speak out. If you start speaking

> *Faith is released when we speak it out.*

negatively, agreeing with the doubt, talking about how big the problem is, then you're giving life to the wrong things. Your words can keep you from your destiny.

In the Scripture, an angel told a priest named Zechariah that his wife, Elizabeth, was going to have a son and to call him John. Zechariah was surprised because they were too old to have children. He said, "Are you sure this is going to happen? Do you see how old we are?" The angel said, "Yes, Zechariah, it's going to happen. But because you doubted, you will remain silent and not be able to speak until the baby is born." That's how powerful words are. God knew that if Zechariah went around speaking defeat and saying, "We're too old. This doesn't seem possible," that would stop the promise.

God has spoken promises to your spirit that may seem too big and impossible. You don't have the connections, the experience, or the funds. Don't do as Zechariah and start to talk yourself out of the miracle. Get in agreement with God. Dare to declare what He put in your heart. You may be facing an illness, with no signs of you getting well. You're right where Zechariah was. "How can I be healed? The medical report says there's no way." God has done His part; now it's up

> *Are you going to give life to defeat and doubt and talk about how you'll never get well, or are you going to release the miracle?*

to you. Are you going to give life to defeat and doubt and talk about how you'll never get well, or are you going to release the miracle? "Lord, thank You that You are my healer. You can do what medicine can't do." Maybe your dream looks impossible, and the promise God whispered to your spirit seems so unlikely. The odds are against you. It's easy to be negative and dismiss it. "It will never happen." Turn it around. "Father, thank You that You're opening doors that no man can shut. Thank You for putting me at the right place. Thank You that what You promised is on the way."

EAT THE FRUIT OF YOUR WORDS

There will be times when you're saying the right things, speaking faith, but nothing is improving. There's no

sign of things chang-
ing. The Scripture says,
"Hold fast the profes-
sion of your faith." It
implies that something

> *"Hold fast the profession of your faith."*

is trying to take it away. It's like a tug-of-war. The
enemy is on the other side trying to pull away what
God put in your heart. You may have had a sickness
for a long time, but hold fast your profession. Don't get
talked out of it. Keep speaking healing. Keep declaring, "I am healthy. I am whole." If you're in debt, keep
talking about abundance. If you're in a season of trouble, keep talking about favor. If you have an addiction,
keep talking about freedom. Every time you declare
victory, the miracle is getting a little closer. Every time
you say, "I am healed," you're moving toward healing. Every time you say, "I am blessed," you're moving
toward increase and promotion. Every time you say, "I
am free. I am not going to stay bound by this addiction, or by this anger, or by this alcohol," you're moving toward freedom, wholeness, and breakthroughs.
It may not have happened yet, but keep releasing the
miracle. Hold fast your profession.

> *Are you speaking faith-filled words of blessing over yourself, over your children, your health, your finances?*

Words are like seeds. Every time you say them, they're taking root and growing. The Scripture says, "You will eat the fruit of your words." Fruit is not fully developed overnight. It may take a little time, but you will become what you're saying. Are you planting good seeds? Are you speaking faith-filled words of blessing over yourself, over your children, your health, your finances? There are miracles in your mouth.

When all the odds were against us getting the Compaq Center, I just kept declaring, "That facility is ours. God is fighting our battles." I told the congregation, "It won't be long until we're in our new facility." One man came up after a service and said, "I've been out of town and didn't know the deal for the Compaq Center had gone through. Congratulations!" I said, "Well, it hasn't gone through yet officially, but I know it's just a matter of time." You have to talk like it's already happened. Rather than say, "I'm going to be healed one day," say, "Lord, thank You that I am healed." Rather than say, "One day I'm going to be blessed," say, "I am blessed. I am favored. I am prosperous." There may not be any sign of it, but this is what faith is all about. You have to release the miracle in your mouth.

"Joel, this sounds good, but I'm struggling. I can't seem to get ahead." Change what you're saying. You're putting out the wrong seeds. The fruit of those words is lack, not enough, and mediocrity. You have to start declaring, "I am surrounded by favor. Goodness and mercy follow me all the days of my life. Promotion is looking for me. Good breaks are on the way. I'm excited about my future." If you do that, get ready for doors to open that you couldn't open. Get ready for a Compaq Center to come across your path. Get ready for God to show out in your life.

CONTINUALLY SPEAK
THE PROMISES

Psalm 35 says, "Let them continually say, 'Let the Lord be magnified, who takes pleasure in the prosperity of

His children.'" They were supposed to go around continually saying that. It seems as though if they said it once that would be enough. But something powerful happens when you don't go through life talking about how you never get any good breaks, how your back will probably never stop hurting, and you can't seem to get ahead. Instead, all through the day you're saying, "God takes pleasure in prospering me. New doors are opening. My health is improving, and I am strong and energetic. My children are mighty in the land. As for me and my house, we will serve the Lord." When you continually talk like that, you are releasing miracles.

Joseph was the prime minister of Egypt for many years. When he was about to die, he made his family promise that they would take his body out of Egypt and bury him in the Promised Land. The Scripture says, "Joseph was so sure God was going to bring the Israelites out of Egypt, he confidently spoke of it," which was hundreds of years before it happened. As with Joseph, there should be things God puts in your heart that you confidently speak about before they

happen. There's
no sign, no reason,
but deep down in
your spirit, you
know that you're
going to accom-

> *There should be things God puts in your heart that you confidently speak about before they happen.*

plish a dream. You know that your family is going to
be restored. You know that you're going to meet the
right person. Now do your part and confidently speak
of it before it happens—not after, not when things
begin to improve, not when you get the promotion.
When there's no sign of it happening, release the miracle. It's in your mouth.

Psalm 91 says, "I will say of the Lord, 'He is my
refuge and my fortress, my God, in whom I trust.'"
Then it gives a list of the great things that will happen. God will shield you from evil. He will rescue you
from every trap. He will protect you from enemies.
But seven verses later, it puts a condition on it. "If you
say, 'The Lord is my refuge,' and make the Most High
your dwelling, no harm will overtake you. For He will
give his angels charge over you to guard you in all

your ways." It doesn't say, "If you believe He's your refuge" or "If you think He's your shield." No, something supernatural happens when you say it. "God, thank You that You're my protector. Thank You that You're my provider, my healer, my way maker. Thank You that You're bigger than what I'm facing. Thank You that You're bringing my dreams to pass." When you say it, the Creator of the universe goes to work.

Words are powerful. A teenage girl named Mary became pregnant, not by a man, but by a word from God. An angel appeared to her and said, "Mary, you are highly favored. You will conceive and give birth to a son without knowing a man. He will be the Messiah, the Son of the Most High." When God wants to create, He doesn't use material things. He uses words. Mary could have said to the angel, "That's impossible. That's never happened before." Instead she said, "Be it unto me even as you have said." She got in agreement with God. She used her words to confirm what she heard, not to debate what she heard. When God puts a promise

> **When God puts a promise in your heart, just agree.**

in your heart, just agree. The Scripture says, "By His stripes you are healed." Don't debate it. "I don't feel healed. My back is still sore." Just agree. "Lord, thank You that I am healed. Be it unto me even as You have said."

God says that when you keep Him first place, "You will lend and not borrow. You will be above and not beneath. Whatever you touch will prosper and succeed." Don't debate it. "I can't seem to get ahead. I've always struggled. My boss doesn't like me." Turn it around and say, "Father, thank You that I am prosperous. Thank You that I have more than enough. Thank You that I am blessed so I can be a blessing." It's not complicated. Just agree with God. You can't talk defeat and have victory. You can't talk lack and have abundance. You can't talk sickness and have health. The miracle is in your mouth. Get in

> *You can't talk defeat and have victory.*

a habit of speaking faith-filled words, declaring victory and abundance over your future.

GET INTO AGREEMENT WITH GOD

Genesis 1 is the story of creation. It says that when the Earth was without form and void, "God said, 'Let there be light,' and there was light." This happened on the first day of creation. But it wasn't until the fourth day that God created the sun and moon. That means for three days, whether it was a literal day or a day was a thousand years, there was light without the sun or the moon. When God speaks, His words are so powerful that things happen for which there is no explanation. How can you have light when there's

> *When God speaks, His words are so powerful that things happen for which there is no explanation.*

no sun as the source? God is supernatural. When He speaks things over you, there may not be an explanation. Back in 1981, the medical report said my mother had no chance to live. But God says, "You will live and not die." God has the final say. Medically speaking, it can't be explained. The only explanation is that we serve a God who is all-powerful.

Sometimes God will speak things into your spirit that don't make sense. Your mind will tell you, *There's no way. You could never reach that level. You could never be that blessed.* Do as Mary did and get in agreement with God. He can give you light without the sun. He can give you water without rain. He can give you healing when there's no source or explanation in the natural. If you agree with your spirit and declare what God says about you, and not what your mind thinks, then God will do things that are unusual, out of the ordinary. You'll see promotion, increase, healing, and breakthroughs that you can't explain. It's God giving you light without a sun. It's God making things happen that no one thought could happen.

Stay in agreement with God. Don't talk yourself out of it; talk yourself into it. It seems impossible, but join Mary and say, "God, be it unto me even as You have said." Jesus' words caused Lazarus, a dead man, to come back to life. God's words stopped the sun for Joshua. His words parted the Red Sea for the Israelites. His words caused leprosy to disappear and bodies to be healed. His words opened prison doors for the apostle Paul and Silas. His words are going to take you further than you've imagined. His words are about to break chains that have held you back, bring new opportunities, thrust you to levels you've never dreamed.

> *His words are about to break chains that have held you back, bring new opportunities, thrust you to levels you've never dreamed.*

SPEAK TO THE ROCK

When the Israelites were headed to the Promised Land, they were in the desert with no water to drink. God told Moses to take his staff and strike a rock. When he did, water came gushing out. There was no explanation for how it happened. They were in the middle of the desert, and suddenly there was an abundance of fresh, cool water, coming out of a rock. The people were so thrilled. Thirty-nine years later, the Israelites were still in the desert and facing the same situation—no water. This time God told Moses to speak to the rock. However, Moses took his staff out and did it the old way. He struck the rock twice, and water came out. But God said that because Moses didn't obey, because he struck it and didn't speak to it, he would not be allowed to go into the Promised Land.

These two events are symbolic. The first time, when God told Moses to strike the rock, represents the old covenant. It meant keeping all the laws, sacrificing animals over and over to cover the people's sins, working for God's goodness. If they didn't perform all the requirements, they wouldn't be blessed. The second time, when God told Moses to speak to the rock, represents the new covenant that we have received. Jesus is the rock from which the water of life flows out—salvation, healing, freedom, and abundance. In this symbolism, Moses didn't have to strike the rock again because Jesus would be crucified for our sins. After Moses struck it twice, God was saying, "No, the price is going to be paid. Jesus will be crucified." Now we don't have

> *Jesus is the rock from which the water of life flows out—salvation, healing, freedom, and abundance.*

to work for our salvation, try to be good enough, and earn God's love and forgiveness. This new covenant is not based on works; it's based on grace.

You don't have to strike the rock; just speak to the rock. Declare your healing, declare your freedom, declare your dreams are coming to pass. Jesus says, "If you have faith as small as a mustard seed, you can say to this mountain, 'Move from here to there,' and it will move. Nothing will be impossible for you." He ties nothing being impossible to speaking to a mountain. Are you living under the old covenant, thinking you have to strike the rock and make everything happen in your own strength? We're living under a better covenant. Under this new covenant, all you have to do is speak. Speak to the sickness, speak to the depression, speak to the dreams God put in your heart.

Maybe you've been working hard, doing all you can to keep things going. Your heart is to be your best, but it's a struggle. If you start speaking to the things that are stressing you, you're going to come into an anointing of ease where you see the water flow without all the work. Don't do as Moses did and keep striking. God is saying, "I've paid the price. Speak to it." Declare favor, declare you are blessed, declare God's goodness. Those things that are hindering you will begin to supernaturally turn around. Situations where you worked hard and couldn't make it change are going to suddenly improve. What God put in your heart is en route. Ease is coming, favor is coming; increase, breakthroughs, creativity, and ideas. You are close to your miracle. Things you've been believing for—buildings, businesses, contracts, houses—are on the way. Speak to the unborn promises in your spirit, the dreams you think are dead. A birth is in your future. New opportunities, new relationships, and new levels are on the way.

> *Speak to the unborn promises in your spirit, the dreams you think are dead. A birth is in your future.*

The miracle is in your mouth. Get in agreement with God and declare what He put in your heart. Let me help you get started. Speak these words out: "I am blessed. I am prosperous. I am forgiven. I am healthy.

I am free. I have the favor of God. My children are mighty in the land. My family will fulfill our destiny. Dreams are coming to pass. Problems are turning around. New doors are opening. I'm excited about my future. I will become all God created me to be."

CHAPTER TWO

Declare It

*Words of blessing have the power to ignite
something in your spirit, to wake up dreams,
to unleash the favor, the gifts,
and the potential that God put in you.*

Words are so powerful that they have the ability to help set the direction for our lives. When they're spoken over us by someone who has authority, such as a parent, a coach, or a mentor, they can help determine our destiny. The reason some people aren't reaching their potential is that they've never had the blessing spoken over them. They've never had anyone declare what they can become, who God says they are, how they have seeds of greatness.

The prophet Isaiah said, "The Spirit of the Sovereign Lord is upon me for He has anointed me to declare the year of the Lord's favor, to announce freedom to the captives, the recovery of sight to the blind, good news to the poor." Isaiah went around declaring favor, freedom, joy, and victory in words that foreshadowed the coming Christ. All those who would receive these blessings, those who would let those words take root, would see it come to pass. Hundreds of years later, Jesus was in a synagogue in Nazareth. He picked up a scroll that had the writings of Isaiah. Of all the hundreds of different passages He could have read, He found this same passage and read to the people: "The Spirit of the Lord is upon Me for He has anointed Me to declare the year of God's favor." Then He ended it by saying He was the fulfillment of this prophecy, that He was the One who had been anointed to bring these promises to pass.

Jesus knew the power of declaring the blessing. He knew that you have to hear victory spoken over you. He knew that you have to hear abundance, healing, and freedom for the blessing to come to pass. He knew that life happens, and it may have taken your passion. You go through disappointments. A dream didn't work out, you're still believing you will meet the right person, and doubts come. *It's never going to happen. You're never going to get well. You've seen your best days.* The negative thoughts start to drown out what was spoken over you. That's why you need a fresh blessing. You need fresh favor spoken over your life. You need a fresh anointing.

That's what I'm going to do in this chapter. Just as Isaiah declared the blessing in his day, and just as Jesus knew it was so important that He repeated it at the very beginning of His ministry, I'm going to declare some things that God says about you. If you let these words take root, if you receive them into your spirit, they are going to put you on a path to greater joy, better health, stronger relationships, and new levels of your destiny. These words have the power to ignite something in your

> *If you let these words take root, if you receive them into your spirit, they are going to put you on a path to greater joy, better health, stronger relationships, and new levels of your destiny.*

spirit, to wake up dreams, to unleash the favor, the gifts, and the potential that God put in you.

IT IS YOUR YEAR OF GOD'S FAVOR

When Jesus chose His disciples, they were ordinary people, working as fishermen, a tax collector, and a zealot, among other common occupations. Yet He looked at them and said, "You are the light of the world. You are the salt of the earth." I can imagine them thinking, *Who's He talking about? There's nothing special about us. He has the wrong people*, but down in their spirits something ignited, something came alive. Their seeds of greatness began to take root, and they felt faith rising up and destiny calling them. Instead of talking themselves out of it, they got in agreement. "Yes, we are the light of the world. Yes, we're going to leave our mark. We're going to impact our generation." Jesus spoke the blessing and declared favor and influence over them, and because they agreed, they saw it come to pass. Two thousand years later, they are still affecting us.

Don't talk yourself out of this favor. Don't think of all the reasons why this can't happen for you. The blessing I'm about to declare is more powerful than any force that's trying to hold you back. The blessing is not cancelled out because of your background, how you were raised, or your education.

> *The blessing is a supernatural empowerment, a divine favor that will thrust you where you can't go on your own.*

It's not stopped by mistakes you've made, by how long it's been, or by disappointments. The blessing is a supernatural empowerment, a divine favor that will thrust you where you can't go on your own.

I declare for you and your family that this will be a year of God's favor. I declare that new doors are going to open, opportunities are going to find you, and good breaks are going to track you down. The right people, divine connections, are going to show up who will use their influence to help you go further. They have been ordained to help you reach your destiny. You don't have to make this happen. You don't have to manipulate things and try to convince others. God has already lined up the right people for you.

In the Old Testament, Ruth was out in the harvest fields picking up leftover wheat. She was a young widow, taking care of her widowed mother-in-law, Naomi, struggling to survive. I'm sure she was discouraged, thinking life was all downhill from there. But the Scripture says the owner of the field noticed Ruth and wanted to be good to her. Ruth didn't see him, but he saw her and suddenly had the desire to help her. God has people in your life who you can't

> *God has people in your life who you can't see right now, but they've seen you.*

see right now, but they've seen you. He's already given them a desire to be good to you, to show you favor, to open a door, to help you get through a challenge. That man didn't just help Ruth. He fell in love with her, and they ended up getting married. You may have been through disappointments, things that haven't worked out, but I declare, as with Ruth, things are about to turn in your favor. I declare that unexpected blessings are on the way. You're going to see good breaks that you didn't see coming, promotion when you weren't next in line, problems turning around when there was no sign of it.

Ruth thought she would have to labor for the rest of her life to survive. She never dreamed that one day she wouldn't be working in the field, but that she would own the field. God has good breaks in your future that are going to catapult you to a new level. Blessings are going to thrust you into influence, resources, and ability that you never imagined. I'm declaring the year of God's favor. Take the limits off God and take

the limits off yourself.
Quit telling yourself
all the reasons why you
can't accomplish your
dreams, telling yourself

> *Take the limits off God and take the limits off yourself.*

what you don't have and what you didn't get. It's not
going to happen just by your ability, your talent, or
your connections. It's going to happen by the Spirit of
the living God. He's breathing on your life right now.
His favor is surrounding you in a greater way. There
are breakthroughs already en route. Healing, pro-
motions, contracts, and the right people are already
headed your way. Now don't talk yourself out of it.
Receive the blessing. "Lord, I believe that this is a year
of favor just as You declared. Thank You that You are
taking me where I can't go on my own."

IT'S NOT TOO GOOD TO BE TRUE

There was an older lady in the Scripture who had been
unable to have children her whole life. She and her
husband had plenty of resources, a nice house, and

influential friends. Life was good except for one thing; she was childless. She and her husband were friends with the prophet Elisha, who would stay at their house when he was in their town. One day Elisha had the desire to be good to this lady. He had known her for a while, but suddenly he wanted to do something special to repay her for her many kindnesses. God knows how

> *God knows how to put desires in people's hearts to be good to you.*

to put desires in people's hearts to be good to you. When you keep doing the right thing and honoring God, He'll line up the right people to help you. Elisha said to this lady, "By this time next year, you're going to have a baby in your arms." She nearly passed out. She responded, "Elisha, don't give me false hopes! I'm an old woman. My husband is older than me. It's not possible for me to have a baby." Her mind said there was no way, but down in her spirit, she was excited. She received the blessing. A year later, just as God promised, she was holding her baby boy. What she thought was too good to be true became a reality. People often tell us that if it seems too good to be true, then it probably is. That may be good advice in one sense, but when it comes to what God says, you have to have the boldness to believe it. "God, this seems too good to be true, but I know You're a supernatural God. You created the universe. You can make things happen that I could never make happen."

You may have dreams that you've given up on. It seems too late. You think you could never get well, never start the business, never see your family restored. That would be too good to be true. But God is saying, "Get ready. By this time next year, you're going to see it come to pass." By this time next year, you're going to have the baby you've been dreaming about. You've been lonely for a long time, and you've accepted that's the way it's always going to be. By this time next year, you're going to meet someone better than you've imagined. You tried to start a business, but nothing worked out, nobody would help you. You think you've missed your chance, but by this time next year, it's going to be up and running. Things are going to fall into place. You've struggled with a sickness for a long time and accepted that you have to live with it. I declare that by this time next year, you're going to be healthy and whole. You're going to feel better than you've ever felt. You're going to run and not be weary, you're going to walk and not faint. The anxiety and the depression seem permanent. By this time next year, you're going to be free. There's going to be great joy in your life. God is turning your mourning into dancing, and your sorrow into joy.

When Job was in the middle of the greatest battle of his life, having lost his health, his family, and his business, he thought he was done. But as he was sitting in the ashes, one of his friends said, "God will once again fill your mouth with laughter." That seemed unbelievable. I'm sure Job thought, *What is he talking about. I'll never laugh again. My world has fallen apart.* But down deep he let those words of encouragement take root. "This is not the end. God is still on the throne. He has the final say." In the midst of his suffering, Job eventually looked up and said, "I know that my Redeemer lives." Instead of complaining, he was saying, in effect, "God, if You declare there will be great laughter in my house, even though it seems too good to be true, I'm bold enough to believe it." Some scholars say that Job's season of trial only lasted nine months. You may

have things com-
ing against you
in your health,
your finances, or
your relationships.
Receive this into
your spirit: By this
time next year, it's

> *What you thought*
> *was permanent is only*
> *temporary. What looks too*
> *big, you will defeat. What*
> *seems impossible, you will*
> *accomplish.*

going to be a different story. What you thought was
permanent is only temporary. What looks too big, you
will defeat. What seems impossible, you will accomplish. How can this happen? There is a blessing on
your life. You are in the year of God's favor. As Jesus
did, I'm announcing freedom for the captives. I'm
declaring that good news is coming to those who are
struggling. The struggle is not how your story ends.
By this time next year, you're going to see God turn
it around.

Your mind may tell you, *This is too good to be true.*
That's what the lady thought when Elisha told her she
was going to have a baby. If she had stayed negative
and doubting, she would have stopped the promise.
What God is speaking over you may seem too good to

be true. It's hard for you to accept how it could happen. The right attitude is: *God, I don't see a way, but I know You have a way. If You declare it, I'm going to receive it. I believe it's my year of favor. I believe that by this time next year, You're going to show out in my life. You're going to take me where I couldn't go on my own. You're going to free me from things that look permanent.*

BREAK GENERATIONAL FORCES

Maybe you're struggling with an addiction. You've tried to stop, with no success. People have told you that you'll always be addicted. It's been in your family line for generations. This is a new day. I declare that you are free. What's held you back in the past will not hold you back any longer. This is a year for breakthroughs. Chains are being loosed right now. Strongholds are coming down. You're about to step into freedom

> *What's held you back in the past will not hold you back any longer. This is a year for breakthroughs.*

that you've never seen. What used to be a struggle is about to get easier. The desire for that addiction is going to get less and less. Its power over you has come to an end. The Scripture says, "The strength of the wicked is being cut off, and the power of the godly has been increased." The strength of what's coming against you has been cut off. Now speak this blessing over your life every day. "Father, thank You that I am free. Thank You that this addiction does not control me. I will become all You've created me to be."

I talked to a lady who is in her forties and has struggled with an addiction since she was in her teens. She told how others in her family had the same addiction. For her whole life she had been told, "You'll always be addicted. It runs in our family." It looked as though that negative cycle would continue. Then someone sent her a link to one of my podcasts and she started listening. She heard me talking about how you weren't created to be addicted, and how that's not who you are, that's what you do. Who you are is a child of the Most High God. You were created to be free. When she heard that, something came alive inside. Those words of faith ignited the freedom in her spirit. She had never had anyone speak the blessing over her. No one had ever declared freedom for the captives to her. For years all she had heard were negative words, what she couldn't do, how she was limited, how she'd never measure up. This day was a turning point.

Every morning, this lady started saying, "I am free. This addiction is not my destiny." She started seeing herself differently. Instead of seeing herself as struggling and addicted, she saw herself as healthy, whole, and free. After three months, she woke up one morning and had no desire for the addiction. It didn't happen gradually; suddenly she was free. This all happened because someone spoke the blessing over her. When I declared freedom, she did her part and received it into her spirit. If you just read these words, they'll encourage and help you for a few days. But if you let them take root in your spirit, if you get

> *If you just read these words, they'll encourage and help you for a few days. But if you let them take root in your spirit, if you get in agreement and say, "Yes, this is for me," they will become a reality.*

in agreement and say, "Yes, this is for me," they will become a reality.

As was true for her, some of the negative things we struggle with have been in our family line for generations. The addictions, the depression, or the bad relationships keep getting passed down. I talked to a man who had a problem with his temper. He said, "Joel, I get angry so easily. I don't know what's wrong with me." He said that his father was the same way, and his grandfather was very hot-tempered. These spirits can get in our family lines and travel from generation to generation. Within some families, you see divorce after divorce. You look back generations and see a pattern where practically every family member went through a divorce. It's not a coincidence that we struggle in certain areas.

Maybe you can't seem to get ahead. You take one step forward, and it's two steps backward. Just when you're ready to move up, you have an unexpected expense. Something goes wrong that takes your savings. It's always something. That's not just bad luck. There are generational forces that are limiting you. They are keeping you from stepping into the abundance and victory that belongs to you. This will continue into the next generation and the next until someone rises up and puts an end to it. I believe that someone is you. You wouldn't be reading this if you weren't called to make a difference. You've been raised up for such a time as this. I declare that every generational curse that's in your family line is broken. In the name of Jesus, I declare that the forces behind the addictions, depression, divorce, low self-esteem, poverty, and not having enough will no longer have any power over you. I declare that you are the difference maker. I declare that you will set a new standard, that you will take your family to a higher level. I declare supernatural favor, supernatural breakthroughs, supernatural increase.

TUNE OUT ALL THE NEGATIVE VOICES

My father was raised in poverty. His parents lost everything during the Great Depression. For a time he had to drop out of high school to work on the farm to help the family survive. It didn't look as though he had much of a future. But at seventeen years old, he gave his life to Christ, the first one in his family. He suddenly had the desire to become a minister. He had no experience, no money, and a poor education, but he told his parents that he was going to leave the farm and go out and start ministering. He could feel the seeds of greatness inside. His parents loved him and were good people, but they didn't understand him. They said, "John, you're making a big mistake. All you know how to do is work on the farm. You better stay here with us." They were saying, in effect, "You don't have what it takes. You're not that talented. We've always been poor, defeated, and mediocre. That's just who we are. That's who you are." If my father would have taken those words into his spirit, I wouldn't be writing this book.

To receive the blessing, you have to get rid of the negative things that people have spoken over you. They may have meant well and were trying to help, but they told you what you can't do, how you don't measure up, and how you'll never be successful. Perhaps an ex-spouse told you that you're not attractive and nobody will

> *To receive the blessing, you have to get rid of the negative things that people have spoken over you.*

ever want you. Don't let them limit your future. They don't know what's in you. They didn't see you before you were formed in your mother's womb. They didn't breathe life into you. They didn't call you, equip you, or empower you. God is saying, "You are blessed. You are favored. You are strong, talented, valuable, and free. You have greatness in you. You are destined to leave your mark, to make the world a better place. You're about to shine. You're about to see favor in greater ways. You've celebrated others, but you're about to be celebrated. You've admired friends and honored coworkers, and you're about to be admired, esteemed, and honored. You're going to come out of the background into the foreground, from being overlooked to being in charge."

I declare that you will excel, you will rise higher, you will go further than anyone thought, and you will accomplish more than you've ever dreamed. You may feel stuck in your career, as though you can't get ahead, but I declare that you're about to be unstuck. You're about to step into opportunity that you've never imagined. You're

> *No person, no bad break, and no disappointment can stop what God has declared. The blessing always overrides the curse.*

going to discover things in you that you never knew you had—gifts, talents, books, songs, movies, ideas, inventions, businesses. Now do your part and tune out all the negative voices. No person, no bad break, and no disappointment can stop what God has declared. The blessing always overrides the curse.

Gaylord Perry was a star baseball pitcher who spent twenty-four years in the major leagues, most of them with the San Francisco Giants. He's in the Hall of Fame, one of the best pitchers of all time. Although Perry was a great pitcher, he was a terrible hitter, averaging less than half the hits of other pitchers. In 1964, his manager, Alvin Dark, was so frustrated with his hitting that he told a newspaper reporter, somewhat kiddingly, "Mark my word. A man will land on the moon before Perry ever hits a home run." His coach declared how bad of a hitter he was. Perry continued to struggle, year after year. Five years later, on July 20, 1969, Neil Armstrong and "Buzz" Aldrin set foot on the moon. History was made. That same night Perry was pitching against the Dodgers. During the third inning, the announcer asked everyone to stand and have a moment of thanks for the astronauts who landed on the moon. A few minutes later, Perry stepped up to the plate and hit the first home run of his career. His manager's words became a prophecy. I wonder how many more home runs Perry would have hit if he hadn't let those words limit his life. Are you being held back by negative words that people have spoken over you? How much further will you go if you tune out

> *Are you being held back by negative words that people have spoken over you?*

what they said and receive what God says about you? He says you're about to step into new levels of favor, that you're about to go where you've never gone, that what's stopped you in the past will not stop you anymore. Now get in agreement with God.

RECEIVE THE BLESSING

In the Old Testament, the Israelites understood the power of the blessing. When a father was getting up there in years, he would call his children in and speak words of life and victory over them. Those words would literally help set the course for their lives. Without the blessing, they knew they couldn't accomplish their dreams, they couldn't go as far as they should. The firstborn blessing was so valuable and so life-changing that Jacob tricked his father, Isaac, into giving him this blessing rather than to his twin brother, Esau, who was the firstborn. Isaac was partially blind and was deceived into thinking he was speaking the double portion blessing over Esau rather than Jacob. When Esau came in and wanted the blessing, Isaac realized he had been tricked and began to tremble uncontrollably. He told Esau, "I've spoken the blessing, and I cannot take it back."

Maybe you've never had anyone speak the blessing over you. Perhaps your father wasn't around. The people who raised you didn't encourage you, and nobody was there to tell you what you could become. Sometimes

> *Tune out every negative, derogatory, hurtful word that was spoken over you and receive these new words into your spirit.*

they did the opposite. All you heard was what you can't do, how you'll never be successful, and how you're not that talented. First, you have to let all that go. Tune out every negative, derogatory, hurtful word that was spoken over you and receive these new words into your spirit. I am going to declare what your Heavenly Father says about you:

"I declare by the authority God has given me that you are blessed. I declare that you are blessed with wisdom, that you have clear direction, that you make good choices in life. I declare that you are blessed with courage, with strength, with great vision, with an obedient heart, and with a positive outlook. I declare that you are blessed with good health, with vitality, with energy, and that you will live a long, satisfied life. I declare that you are blessed with a good family, good friends, healthy relationships, and that your children will be mighty in the land. I declare that you are blessed with protection, that God is guarding you, guiding you, and that angels are watching over you and your family.

"I declare that you are blessed with promotion, with good success, with ideas, with creativity. I declare that whatever you put your hands to will prosper. You will be blessed in the city and blessed in the country. You will be blessed when you come in and blessed when you go out. I declare that you will lend and not borrow; you will be above and never beneath. I declare that every negative word, every curse that has been spoken over you, is broken. I declare that negative things that have been in your family line for generations will no longer have any effect on you. The generational curse is broken, and the generational blessing is beginning.

"I declare that this will be a year of God's favor, freedom from every bad habit, recov-

> *"I declare that you are blessed."*

ery from everything that was lost. I declare that from this day forward, you will experience a new sense of freedom, a new happiness, a new fulfillment. I declare that you are blessed."

CHAPTER THREE

Tell Yourself a New Story

When you get what you believe about yourself in line with what God says, things will happen that you couldn't make happen.

We all have a story of how we see ourselves and how we see our future. It comes from how we were raised, what people have said about us, our successes and failures. Perhaps you have a negative story. "I've been hurt too much. I can't love again." "My family is at a disadvantage. I'll never be successful." "I have big dreams, but I don't have the talent or the experience." You know what's stopping you? Your story. You're being limited by what you're telling yourself. What you believe about yourself and how you see your circumstances is the story that you've written. That story will override what anyone else says. It's even more powerful than the facts. You can be incredibly gifted and have a great personality, but if you tell yourself that you're average and don't have much to offer, your gifts won't come out as they should. Is the story you're telling yourself keeping you from rising higher? Why don't you tell yourself a new story?

The Scripture says, "God is the author and

> *Why don't you tell yourself a new story?*

finisher of your faith." He's the author. Psalm 139 says, "All of your days were written before you were born." God has already written your story. The key is to get your story in line with His story. God says that His plans for you are for good, to give you a future and a hope. He calls you a masterpiece, valuable, victorious, an overcomer. He says, "What was meant for harm, I'm turning to your advantage." You may have been through bad breaks, things that are unfair. The enemy would love to take that and rewrite what God says about you and become the author of your story. You need to take the pen back, cross out all the lies, and tell yourself a new story. God says that He has beauty for ashes, that He will pay you back for the wrongs. You wouldn't be alive unless He has something awesome in front of you. Don't let circumstances, what didn't work out, or what you don't think you have convince you to live with a wrong story. Your story is setting the limits for your life.

Quit telling yourself that you'll never be successful, never get out of debt, never meet the right person. Tell yourself a new story. "I'm made in the image of God. I'm crowned with favor. I'm a masterpiece. There is greatness in me. Whatever I touch prospers and succeeds. Blessings are chasing me down. My latter

> *Have you let people, circumstances, doubt, and negativity rewrite your story?*

days will be better than my former days." That's the story God has written about you. Is your story contradicting His story? Have you let people, circumstances, doubt, and negativity rewrite your story? Don't let someone else become the author. Take the pen back and tell yourself a new story.

WHO SAYS YOU CAN'T DO IT?

When my father went to be with the Lord in 1999, I knew I was supposed to step up and pastor the church. The problem was that the wrong story was playing in my mind. For years I had told myself, *I can't get up and speak in front of people. I'm too quiet. I don't have the training or the right personality. I won't know what to say.* Other thoughts said, *Joel, look at your father. He was strong, bold, and outgoing. He had a lot of experience. No one is going to listen to you.* I had to do what I'm asking you to do. I started telling myself a new story. I went back to the One who had written my story, the One who breathed life into me, the One who knew me before I was formed in my mother's womb. I said, "God, I'm going to let You be the author of my story. I'm going to believe that I'm strong in the Lord and in the power of Your might. I believe that I can do all things through Christ. I believe that I'm equipped, empowered, and anointed. Lord, thank You that my gifts will come out to the full. Thank You that You have raised me up for such a time as this." When you get your story in line with what God says, things will happen that you couldn't make happen. I wouldn't be where I am today if I had not told myself a new story. You wouldn't be reading this if I had let that fear, intimidation, and insecurity keep playing.

> **Don't let the wrong story keep you from your greatness.**

Don't let the wrong story keep you from your greatness.

"Well, Joel, I can't lead my department. I

can't get up in front of people and talk. I'm not that talented." Who told you that? Where did that story come from? Could it be that a wrong story is keeping you from rising higher? "I can't make A's in school. I'm not that smart. All I can make are C's." You have to realize that the enemy has taken the pen and rewritten your story. "I can't break this addiction. I'll never get out of this neighborhood. I'll never accomplish my dream. It's too late." As long as you believe that story, it's going to become a reality. God didn't create you to just get by, to just survive life. He created you to excel, to leave your mark. He said that you are to reign in life. Victory starts in your mind. The Scripture says, "Be careful how you think, because your thoughts run your life." Your story is setting the limits for your life.

> *Your story is setting the limits for your life.*

After Moses had been living as a shepherd in the desert for forty years, God came to him and said, "Moses, go and tell Pharaoh to let My people go." Moses responded, "God, I can't stand before Pharaoh. I stutter. I have a problem with my speech. You know that I don't speak well." God asked Moses, "Who made your tongue? Who made your mouth?" Do you think God would ask you to do something and then not give you the ability to do it? Do you think He would choose you to be here at this time in history and not give you everything you need to live a victorious life, to overcome obstacles, to leave your family better off than they were before? What was Moses' problem? He had the wrong story. He was telling himself, "I'm unqualified. I'm at a disadvantage. I have these limitations." The story you believe is the story that's going to come to pass.

Don't tell God what you can't do. "God, I can't get well. You saw the report." "I can't start my own business. I'm not that talented." "I can't do something significant. I come from the wrong family." If you say you can't, God will say to you what He said to Moses: "Who made you? Who wrote your story? Who gave you your gifts?

> *The Creator of the universe, the God who spoke worlds into existence, is your author. He's written your story.*

Who picked out your family? Who lined up your good breaks? Who planned out your days?" The Creator of the universe, the God who spoke worlds into existence, is your author. He's written your story. You're not doing life on your own. Go back to what He says about you.

DELETE THE OLD STORY

It's interesting that as little children we start off with big dreams. We're going to be an astronaut, a designer, an architect, a scientist, or a singer. A little boy recently told me that he was going to design airplanes. He seemed to know everything about avionics, the electronic systems used on aircraft. As children, we have no limits. We believe we can do great things. But over time our dreams start to get watered down. People tell us what we can't do. We go through disappointments, things that are unfair, and life starts to rewrite our story. We let the negative taint how we see ourselves and what we're capable of. We end up settling for so much less than what God has for us. Pay attention to the story you're telling yourself. Go back to what God put in your heart. He wants you to dream again, to believe again, to love again. Don't let a wrong story limit your destiny. Don't believe the lies that say, "Just live with the sickness and depression. You'll never get well. You'll never go to college. You'll never meet the right person. You better hope that you can just make it through life." Tell yourself a new story. You can still accomplish your dream. You can still get well. You can still meet someone who's awesome. You can still go to new levels. Delete the old story. Get rid of the limited thinking. That's what's stopping the new things that God has in store for you.

This is the mistake the Israelites made. God brought them out of slavery in Egypt, parted the Red Sea, and led them toward the Promised Land. It was a great day. Their dreams were coming to pass. They were finally free. But the problem was that they still saw themselves as slaves. They saw themselves as always being at a disadvantage. "We've been through too much." Every time they faced opposition, they either complained or were afraid. When they came near to the Promised Land, God told them He would give them the victory, but they said, "Moses, the people are too big. We don't have a chance. Let's go back to Egypt. Let's go back to being slaves." Notice how powerful a wrong story is. After being in slavery, mistreated, and abused for their entire lives, they wanted to go back to that same environment. They came out of Egypt, but Egypt never came out of them. If you don't change the story you're telling yourself, you'll

> *They came out of Egypt, but Egypt never came out of them.*

go back to things that don't make sense. God delivered them from the Pharaoh, gave them manna to eat every morning, and brought water out of a rock. They saw His awesome power firsthand. It seemed as though it would have been so logical, so easy for them to say, "This is a new day. God has done great things. We're free. He promised to give us this land. Let's go in." Instead, they kept their slave mentality. The story they told themselves was: "We'll always be defeated. This is our lot in life."

But I love the fact that the children of these Israelites, the next generation, had a different story. Their attitude was: *We've seen the suffering, the mistreatment, and the years of wandering through the desert. That may be what our parents accepted, but that is not our story. We are going into the Promised Land. We're going to eat the fruit. We're going to live in houses that we didn't build and enjoy the blessings God has in store for us.* Their parents saw themselves as slaves; these children saw themselves as sons and daughters of the Most High God. They knew they were not at a disadvantage but were surrounded by His favor.

Forty years after their parents turned around from the Promised Land and wandered in the desert, these children went into that same land, defeated the opposition, and lived there in a place of abundance. The difference was the story they told themselves. Their parents could have gone in. They could have enjoyed years of God's favor, but

> *Don't let a wrong story— what you've been through, what looks too big, what hasn't happened—convince you that you can't defeat your giants, can't accomplish your dream, can't be healthy, successful, and fulfilled.*

they let their doubts, their fears, and the opposition rewrite their story. Don't do as these parents did. Don't let a wrong story—what you've been through, what looks too big, what hasn't happened—convince you that you can't defeat your giants, can't accomplish your dream, can't be healthy, successful, and fulfilled. The enemy took your pen. He's altering the story God wrote for you. Get that pen back. Cross out all the lies.

DON'T LET OTHER PEOPLE PUT THEIR STORY ON YOU

In the previous chapter, I wrote about what it was like when my father was growing up, and I want to expand on that. The story he was told growing up, and the story he saw modeled, was: "We're poor. We'll never do anything significant. The odds are against us." Having lost everything in the Great Depression, his parents were doing their best to survive. I recognize that tough times come, and life can throw us curves. You may be in poverty, but don't ever let poverty get in you. Don't develop a poor mind-set that says all you can believe for is just enough to get by. Don't accept that as your destiny. God has an abundant life for you. He knows how to make streams in the desert, how to bring you out of struggle and lack, how to give you a bountiful life. But you may need to change the story that you're telling yourself.

When my father was seventeen years old and gave his life to Christ, even though everything said that he had no real future, something came alive inside. He made a decision that his children would never be raised in the poverty and lack that he was raised in. He started telling himself a new story. Instead of saying, "You're stuck in this environment. You'll never get ahead, never make anything of your life," his attitude was: *I'm destined to do great things. The favor of God is on my life. He will open doors that no person can shut and take me where I can't go on my own.*

When he told his parents that God was calling him to become a minister and that he was leaving home to go out and start speaking, they did all they could to persuade him to not try. They were certain he would fail. They meant well, but you can't let other people put their story on you. Don't let their defeat, their negativity, or their limited vision keep you from believing that you can rise higher. People are not the author of

> *People are not the author of your story. God is.*

your story. God is. He called you, He anointed you, and He put the dreams in you. Other people may not understand. They may try to talk you into watering down your dream. Keep the right story playing in your mind. My father left that day and started on a journey that was more fulfilling and more rewarding than he ever imagined. He ministered for over fifty years and saw God's favor in amazing ways.

As was true with my father, perhaps the environment you were raised in has tainted your story. The people you grew up around didn't believe for much. Perhaps the people who you're with now accept mediocrity. You have to be the one to break out of the rut. Don't let that negative story limit your life. That was fine for them, but this is a new day. God wants you to go further. He has things in your future that are much greater than you can imagine. Now get in agreement with Him. Quit telling yourself that you're limited, that you've gone as far as you can, that you'll always struggle. No, tell yourself a new story. Have an abundant mentality. Speak the blessing and say, "Lord, thank You that my cup runs over. Thank You that I live under the open windows of Heaven, that You take pleasure in prospering me, and that I will leave an inheritance to my children's children."

YOUR STORY MAY BE TOO LIMITING

I read about a bear that had been forced to live for years in a twelve-foot-by-twelve-foot cage in an overseas zoo. During the day, she would pace back and forth, back and forth, hour after hour. One day she was rescued by government authorities who made arrangements for her to be relocated in a bear sanctuary that provided a spacious area, with big pools of water, rocks on which to climb, and green grass everywhere you looked. It was like a dream setting. They transported the bear into her new home and were so excited to open the cage, but she wouldn't come out. Finally, they had to push her out and onto the green grass. They thought that eventually she'd take off running and explore the new surroundings, but all she ever did was pace in a circle of her imaginary cage. She never went to the pools, never climbed the rocks, never played with the other bears. She got out of the cage, but the cage never got out of her. Her story was: "I'm stuck. I'm limited. I can't go any farther." But the truth was that she had a whole field to play in.

The story you tell yourself is very powerful. How you were raised, what you saw modeled, and the environment you're in can create boundaries in your mind that you adapt to as that bear did. Even though God has all kinds of amazing things in store, if you tell yourself that you've reached your limits, that you can't get well, that you can't accomplish a dream, you'll miss the fullness of your destiny. The story you tell yourself is the story that's going to come to pass. My encouragement is that the cage is open. God has a big life for you. He has favor, opportunities, and great relationships for you. Get

> *The story you tell yourself is the story that's going to come to pass.*

in agreement with Him. Tell yourself a new story. You don't have to figure out how it's going to happen. All you have to do is believe.

In Mark 5, there was a lady who had been sick with an issue of blood for twelve years. She had gone to the best doctors, spent all her money, but nothing had helped. The story she was telling herself was: "This sickness is permanent. There's nothing more that I can do. It's just my bad luck." She continued to suffer and go downhill. But one day she heard that Jesus was passing through her town. Despite how weak she felt, despite the circumstances, she told herself a new story. She said, "When I touch the edge of His robe, I'm going to be healed." The Scripture says, "She kept saying to herself, 'I'm going to get well. Healing is coming. Things are about to change.'" She deleted her old story and started telling herself a new story. Faith began to rise in her heart. As she kept saying that healing is coming, she made her way through the crowd, touched Jesus' robe, and was healed instantly.

As with this lady, you may have a good reason to have a negative story. You may be facing a challenge in your health, in your finances, or in a relationship. It's easy to let defeated thoughts, "can't do it" thoughts, "it's never going to work out" thoughts, play in your mind. That's when you have to do as she did and dig down deep and say, "No, I'm deleting this story. I will be the exception. I will get well. I will see my family restored. I will break this addiction. I will lend and not borrow. I will accomplish my dream." Give God something to work with. You can't have an old story and see the new things He wants to do. Too often our story is limiting us. What we're telling ourselves is limiting us. We're looking

> *You can't have an old story and see the new things He wants to do.*

at it in the natural, but God is supernatural. This is what faith is all about. That's why God said to Moses, "Who made your tongue?" He was saying, "Moses, you're only looking at your ability. Don't you realize that I have all-power? I created the universe. Nothing can stop My plan from coming to pass."

God has already written your story. Yes, there will be ups and downs, challenges and victories. But there's nothing you'll come up against that He doesn't already have a solution for. He won't let you get in a problem that He can't bring you out of. The key is to not let the wrong story take root. In difficult times, when nothing is changing, when it's taking longer than you thought, it's tempting to get discouraged and bitter and to water down your dreams. You have to keep telling yourself, "This is not permanent. It didn't come to stay; it came to pass. I'm an overcomer. God always causes me to triumph. This is not going to stop me. Blessing is headed my way."

SEE YOURSELF THE WAY GOD SEES YOU

There was an experiment conducted in a high school in California. The principal told three teachers that they had been chosen to lead a new program because they were the highest rated, most effective teachers in the district. Out of the district's thousands of students, the top ninety students were placed in three classes with these teachers. The teachers were told that they were to take the students with the highest IQ and most talent and teach them at a faster pace. The teachers and the students were so excited, knowing that they were the best and brightest. At the end of the school year, these three classes had learned 30 percent more than the other students. They were 30 percent further along in math, reading, and science. It was a huge success. Then the principal informed the teachers that they had not actually had the top ninety students in the district. The students had been randomly chosen. The teachers felt really good about themselves, thinking that they had done such an awesome job and were so smart. Then the principal informed the teachers that they weren't actually the most effective teachers. They were randomly chosen out of a hat.

The point is that when you tell yourself a different story, when you tell yourself that you're made in the image of God, you're going to see new levels of your destiny. When you tell yourself that you're smart, talented, favored, valuable, attractive, and wise, you start to see yourself the way God sees you and become who He says you are. The only thing that's holding some people back is the story they're telling themselves. "I'm not that talented. I'm not as smart as my cousin. I can't

> *Who knows what you can do if you start seeing yourself differently?*

run a business. I can't get the promotion no matter how hard I try." Who knows what you can do if you start seeing yourself differently?

You may think this is funny, but ever since I started ministering over twenty years ago, every time I get up to speak, wherever I go, I think to myself, *Everyone here loves me. Everyone here thinks I'm great.* I know that's being naïve, that not everyone thinks that, but that's the story I tell myself. Do me a favor and leave me in my ignorance. That's a lot better than feeling insecure and intimidated and thinking, *I don't think they're going to like me. They're not going to listen to me. I hope I'm not boring them.* The story I tell myself is: "Joel, you're anointed. You're favored. You're blessed." I don't say that arrogantly, but in humility. The story you need to tell yourself is: "God breathed His life into me. I'm a masterpiece. I have something great to offer this world. I am fearfully and wonderfully made." You are wonderfully made. My brother, Paul, was fearfully made.

LINE YOUR STORY UP WITH
GOD'S STORY

You can't reach your destiny if you're discounting yourself, seeing everyone else as smarter, greater, or prettier. Can I tell you that you're awesome, you're talented, you have a great personality, and you're going to do something amazing? If you don't believe in yourself, it's going to limit your life. Sometimes we have a false sense of humility. "Everyone else is great, and it's just little old me." No, God handpicked you. He chose you to be here. He crowned you with favor. He put gifts in you. No one else has your fingerprints. You're a designer original. You're not better than anyone else, but you're not less than anyone else. Tell yourself a new story: "I am valuable. I am favored. I am attractive. I have a great personality. People like being around me." You have enough people who are against you; don't be against yourself.

Are you telling yourself the right story? "Joel, I stutter. I have this weakness." So did Moses. Who made your tongue? Do you think a limitation is going to keep you from your destiny? Do you think that God

> *Are you telling yourself the right story?*

somehow shortchanged you and you're lacking in some area? Not a chance. "Well, I have this sickness . . . this addiction . . . this problem at work." I'm not saying that you should deny it and act as though it's not there. But as the lady with the issue of blood did, tell yourself a new story. Healing is coming, freedom is coming, breakthroughs are coming. Like that bear, are you living with a limited mentality because of how you were raised or the environment you're in now? I'm telling you that the door is wide open to an abundant life. God has awesome things in your future. Make sure your story lines up with His story, because the story you tell yourself is the story that's going to come to pass. If you do this, I believe and declare that like the children of the Israelites, you're going to go into your promised land. You're going to see favor, overcome obstacles, accomplish dreams, and reach the fullness of your destiny.

CHAPTER FOUR

"You Promised"

If you only tell God what's wrong, and not what He has promised, you're limiting what He can do.

When we face difficulties, one of the best things we can do is find a promise in the Scripture and remind God of what He says about us. "God, You promised that I would lend and not borrow. You promised that my children will be mighty in the land. You promised that with long life You will satisfy me." The prophet Isaiah says, "Put God in remembrance of His promises." He doesn't say to put God in remembrance of your problems. It's easy to complain and say, "God, the people at work aren't treating me right. My back has been hurting, and my kids are getting on my nerves." It's okay to be honest with God, but don't just pray the problem, pray the promises.

If you only tell God what's wrong, you're limiting what He can do. Follow up the problem with a promise. "God, my back has been hurting, but You promised that You would restore health to me. Thank You that healing is coming." "God, my coworkers are trying to make me look bad and not giving me any credit for my work, but You promised that You would be my vindicator. You promised that the enemy would fall

> *God is not obligated to bring to pass what we say, but He is obligated to bring to pass what He says.*

into the trap they set for me, so I'm going to stay in peace and let You fight my battles." "God, my dream looks impossible. I don't have the connections, the funding, or the experience." If you stop there, you'll get stuck. Follow up the problem with the promise. "But, God, You promised that Your favor surrounds me like a shield. You promised that whatever I touch will prosper and succeed. You promised that You are opening doors that no man can shut. Thank You that You are taking me where I can't go on my own." God is not obligated to bring to pass what we say, but He is obligated to bring to pass what He says. When He hears His promises coming out of your mouth, angels go to work, forces of darkness are pushed back, and favor is released in a new way.

When Isaiah says to put God in remembrance of His promises, it's not because God has forgotten what He said. It's not for His sake; it's for our sake. God knows that when you start declaring His promises, when you start speaking what He says about you, not only is faith going to rise in your heart, but it's going to change your perspective. You won't go around with a victim mentality; you'll have a victor mentality. You'll know that God being for you is more than the world being against you. You'll know that sickness is no match for our God. You'll know that trouble at work can't stop your purpose.

Most of us have the first part down. We're good at telling God our problems, but you have to follow it up with a "You promised." The more you talk about the promises, the less you'll talk about your problems. I start every morning thanking God for what He promised over my life. "Father, thank You that You promised that the path of the righteous gets brighter and brighter. You promised that no good thing will You withhold because I walk uprightly. You promised

If you're spending more time talking about your problems than you are the promises, that's out of balance.

that You would do exceedingly abundantly above and beyond what I can imagine." If you're spending more time talking about your problems than you are the promises, that's out of balance. Maybe you're not seeing things turn around, not seeing increase, promotion, and healing because you're putting God in remembrance of the wrong things. You're telling Him what wasn't fair, who offended you, and how bad the medical report is. Try a different approach. Take a break from telling God everything that's wrong. He already knows your needs. There's nothing wrong with asking, but at some point you need to switch over to thanking Him for what He's promised.

GOD MOVES WHEN
HE HEARS HIS WORD

My sister Lisa and her husband, Kevin, tried for years to have a baby without success. Lisa went through fertility treatments, had a couple of surgeries, and did everything she could. Finally, the doctors said there was nothing more they could do, that Lisa and Kevin wouldn't be able to have children. Lisa could have been depressed and told God how bad it was and begged Him to give her children. Instead, she made a list of all the promises that God made concerning children. She typed them out and put them up on her bathroom mirror. It says in the Scripture that God will make the barren woman a happy mother of children. It says that children are a heritage from the Lord. Psalm 128 says that your children will be like olive shoots around your table. The book of Deuteronomy says that the fruit of your womb will be blessed.

All through the day, instead of complaining and praying the problem, "God, You heard that the doctors said I can't have children. It's not fair," Lisa was praying the promises, "Father, thank You that You promised You would make me the happy mother of children." It's very powerful when you take it off what you want and put it on what God says. "God, You promised that the fruit of my womb is blessed. You

> *It's very powerful when you take it off what you want and put it on what God says.*

promised my children are a heritage from the Lord."
She did this year after year, with no sign of anything
changing. But the Scripture says, "God watches over
His word to perform it." It doesn't say that God
watches over our complaints or our begging. "Please,
God, You know this is not fair. You have to turn this
around." Yes, He sees the wrongs and is concerned,
but what moves Him to act is when He hears His
Word.

Seven years later, Lisa received a phone call from
a friend who runs a home for teenage girls. This lady
said, "I don't know why I'm calling you, but we have a
young lady who's about to give birth to twin girls. I'm
wondering if you'd be interested in adopting them."
Lisa's husband, Kevin, is a twin. That was always their
dream, that they would have twins. They adopted
those two girls and then another child. Just as God
promised, Lisa is now the happy mother of three children. She says, "God is so good. I have three children,
and I never had to get pregnant." When you pray the
promises, children will find you, the right people will
track you down, good breaks will come your way.

Whatever you're believing for, you need to do as

Lisa did and find some promises. Make a list and put it on your phone, on your bathroom mirror, and on your computer. All through the day, remind God of what He promised you. If you're fighting an illness, it's easy to talk about the sickness, about what the doctor said and how it doesn't look good. Sometimes we know more about the problem than we do the promise. We spend hours searching the Internet, learning about everything that could possibly go wrong. Why don't you spend fifteen minutes and google scriptures that speak the blessing to whatever you're facing? "Father, You promised that You would restore health to me. You promised that I

> *Why don't you spend fifteen minutes and google scriptures that speak the blessing to whatever you're facing?*

would live and not die and declare the works of the Lord. You promised that by the stripes of Your Son Jesus, I was healed." If you've been struggling with an addiction for a long time, you may think it will never change. "Father, You promised that You have destroyed every yoke and broken every bondage. You promised that the enemy I see today I will see no more. You promised that whom the Son sets free is free indeed. So thank You that I am free." That's not just being positive, that's reminding God of what He said.

THE PROMISE WILL BECOME
A REALITY

I know a lady who was at odds with her teenage daughter. She would come for prayer very often during our church services, and she was always upset and discouraged. I tried to cheer her up and convince her to keep believing, but it seemed as though more than coming for prayer she just wanted to tell me how it wasn't changing and how her daughter was disrespectful. I told her what I'm telling you: "Talking about the problem is not doing anything productive. Complaining is not making things better. You need to start reminding God of what He promised you." I gave her the scripture in Proverbs 31 that says, "Children will rise and call their mother blessed." At that time her daughter was calling her every name except "blessed."

This mother started going through the day saying, "Father, You promised that my children will rise up and call me blessed." When her daughter was disrespectful, instead of complaining, thinking about how it wasn't working out, she would say, "Father, thank You that my daughter is going to call me blessed." She found other scriptures. "Father, You promised that children are a gift from You to be enjoyed. Thank You that I will enjoy my daughter, that we will have fun together." She kept doing this month after month, with no sign of things changing. This is what faith is all about. If you can see it, you don't need faith. A few years later, her daughter made a complete turnaround. She was like a different person—kind, loving, and respectful. Today, she and her mother are the best of friends. They do everything together. Now when this mother says, "God, You promised that my children will rise up and call me blessed," she's not saying it by faith. It's become a reality. God fulfilled His promise.

The Scripture says, "God is not a man, that He should lie. Has He ever spoken and failed to act? Has He ever promised and not carried it through?" God has never failed in the past, and He's not going to start

> *God has never failed in the past, and He's not going to start with you. Stay in faith and stay open.*

with you. Stay in faith and stay open. It may not happen your way or on your timetable, but God is true to His Word. When you're constantly saying, "God, You promised," that's what allows Him to bring promises to pass.

I talked to a well-known elderly actor who was very down on himself. He said, "Joel, I'm a has-been. I never get any good roles. I've peaked, and it's all downhill from here." When you speak defeat over your life, you're inviting bad breaks, lack, and disappointments. Zip that up and find a "You promised." "God, You promised that my latter days will be better than my former days. You promised that Your favor is not for a season but for a lifetime. You promised that You will bring me to a flourishing finish." Get in agreement with God. We need you alive and passionate for your whole life.

Maybe you've had some bad breaks. Perhaps you've gone through a loss, somebody walked out of your relationship. You could sit around in self-pity, have a chip on your shoulder, and think, *Why did this happen to me?* That's going to keep you defeated. Turn it around and say, "God, You promised that You would give me beauty for ashes. You promised that weeping endures for a night, but joy comes in the morning. You promised that because I got a double dose of trouble, I would get a double dose of favor. So I thank You that I'm not just coming out, I'm coming out better." When you declare the promises, God will make up for what was unfair. As He did for Joseph, He'll take you from the pit to the palace. As He did for Ruth, He'll take you from working in the field to owning the field. As He did for David, He'll take you from the background to the foreground, from being overlooked to being in charge. Pay attention to what's coming out of your mouth. Are you talking more about the problems or about God's promises? What you're bringing

> **What you're bringing to God's remembrance is going to determine whether or not you reach your destiny.**

to God's remembrance is going to determine whether or not you reach your destiny.

ALL HE ASKS IS THAT YOU BELIEVE

In 2 Kings 7, the Israelites in Samaria were already in a great famine when a Syrian army besieged the city and cut off their food supply. The Syrians were waiting for them to starve so they could come in and take the city without a fight. The prophet Elisha was in the city and said to the Israelites, "By this time tomorrow there will be so much food that you'll be able to buy six quarts of choice flour for only one piece of silver, and twelve quarts of barley grain for only one piece of silver." The officer assisting the king said, "Elisha, that's impossible. We're surrounded by a huge army, we're outnumbered, we have no food, and we're starving. There's no way." Elisha said to him, "It will happen. God has promised it, but because you doubted, you will see it but not eat it."

There were four lepers sitting outside the city gates. They said to one another, "Why should we sit here until we die? There's no food in the city. Let's walk to the enemy's camp and surrender. Perhaps they'll not kill us but have mercy on us and give us food." As they were walking, God multiplied the sound of their footsteps. The Syrian army heard what sounded like a huge army approaching, chariots and horses. They panicked and took off running for their lives, leaving behind all their food, their supplies, and their equipment. The lepers found the Syrian camp was deserted and went back and told the Israelites. The officer who didn't believe Elisha's word was in charge of the city gates. When he opened the gates to let the people out, they were so excited to plunder the Syrian camp that they trampled him to death. He was the only one who didn't get to eat when the promise came to pass.

Now don't make this man's mistake and talk yourself out of what God promised. His attitude should have been: *God, You promised that by tomorrow we're going to have an abundance of food. I don't see how that's possible. There's no way in the natural that this can happen, but I know that You're a supernatural God.* God doesn't ask us to figure it out. All He asks is that we believe. When He puts a promise in your heart,

> *All He asks is that we believe.*

don't think of all the reasons it's not going to work out. Sometimes you have to turn your mind off, so to speak. Faith is not always going to make sense. What God says is not always going to be logical. If you reason it out, check with all the experts, and study all the reports, you'll miss God's best. Dare to believe. Dare to say, "God, I don't see a way, but I know that You have a way."

We think natural, but God is supernatural. He's not limited by what limits us. He controls the universe. In Daniel 3, when He kept the fiery furnace from burning three Hebrew teenagers, that didn't make sense, but He is God. He enabled Sarah to have a baby when she was ninety years old. He pushed back the waters of the Red Sea for the Israelites and took them through on dry ground. He healed my mother of terminal cancer after the doctors sent her home to die. He put me in front to speak to thousands of people when I had no formal training or experience as a pastor. He gave us the Compaq Center for our church facility when all the odds were against us. Don't let your natural logic talk you out of what a supernatural God can do.

> *Don't let your natural logic talk you out of what a supernatural God can do.*

HAVE A CHILDLIKE FAITH

The Scripture talks about how we need to have a childlike faith. Children don't try to figure things out. When you tell your child that you're going to buy them something or take them somewhere, they don't worry about it. They don't wonder if you have the means, and they don't lose sleep over whether it's going to happen. They trust you. When our daughter, Alexandra, was about ten years old, she loved to go to Disneyland. We hadn't been there in a few years. I was putting her to bed one night when she asked, "Dad, can we go to Disneyland again?" I answered almost in passing, "Sure we can." She said, "You promise?" I responded, "Yes, I promise." She smiled real big, then

I kissed her and went to bed. Early the next morning, before I was even out of bed, she came running into our bedroom. She didn't say "Good morning!" or "How are you?" or "I love you." No, she said, "Daddy, when are we going to Disneyland?" It was never *if,* it was *when.* She had so much confidence in me. She knew that I wouldn't break my promise, that it was just a matter of time.

Never once did Alexandra say, "Dad, can I check the finances to see if we can afford to go to Disneyland? Can I study your schedule? What if we can't get flights? What if the hotels are booked? What if something comes up at the church?" She didn't worry about any of the details. She didn't concern herself about how it was going to happen. Why? She knew that her father would take care of that. She knew that I wouldn't have promised if I couldn't deliver it. She also knew that I'm human,

> *What would happen if we had that same kind of trust in our Heavenly Father, knowing that He cannot fail, that He cannot go back on His Word?*

and I could let her down. I could break my promise and not keep my word, yet she had this incredible trust in me. What would happen if we had that same kind of trust in our Heavenly Father, knowing that He cannot fail, that He cannot go back on His Word?

"God, You promised that as for me and my house, we will serve the Lord. You promised that I would lend and not borrow. You promised that I would get well. I'm not going to worry about how it's going to happen. I'm not going to go around stressed because I don't see anything changing. I'm not going to be wondering if it's going to work out, if I'm going to meet the right person, or if I'm going to accomplish my dreams. God, I trust You. I believe You are true to Your Word. In Your perfect timing, and in Your own way, You will bring Your promise to pass." That's a childlike faith. You're not trying to figure out all the details. You're not wondering if He has the funds, if He knows the right people, or what will happen if the obstacle is too big. God controls the universe. He wouldn't have promised it if He wasn't going to bring it to pass.

HE KEEPS HIS PROMISES FOREVER

We see how faithful God is to His promises with David. God told David that one of his descendants would always be on the throne of Israel. Twenty-three years after David died, his son Solomon was on the throne and making poor choices. He married many foreign wives, and then he started worshipping their idols. God said, "Solomon, because of the wrongs that you've done in My sight, I would normally take the kingdom away from you, but I will not do it for the sake of your father, David." God was saying, "Solomon, you knew better and don't deserve mercy. You're off course, but I made a promise to your father, and I am a God who keeps My promises even to a dead man."

Over three hundred years later, another of David's descendants, King Hezekiah, was on the throne and in great danger. An enemy army had surrounded Jerusalem, and it looked as though the people were done. There was no way out. But at the last minute, God sent an angel in the night who wiped out 185,000 of the enemy troops. Hezekiah and all of his people were spared. I can imagine Hezekiah saying, "God, what did we do to deserve Your favor?" God said, "Hezekiah, it's not about what you've done. It's for the sake of my servant David, who's been in the grave for three hundred years. He's dead and gone, but I made a promise to him that one of his descendants would always be on the throne. I'm a God who keeps My promises forever." Maybe you're standing on a promise that hasn't come to pass yet. Don't worry. Your time is coming. If God will go to such great lengths to keep His promises to a man who's dead, how much more will He keep His promise to you? Stay in faith. Keep reminding Him of what He

> *If God will go to such great lengths to keep His promises to a man who's dead, how much more will He keep His promise to you?*

promised, keep bringing it to His remembrance, and keep thanking Him that it's on the way. As David did, you're going to see God show out in your life. You're going to see those promises come to fulfillment.

BE BOLD DESPITE HOW YOU FEEL

In Genesis 32, Jacob was about to meet his brother, Esau, after many years of being completely estranged. Jacob had cheated Esau, stolen his birthright, and tricked their father into giving him the firstborn blessing that belonged to Esau. Esau had been so upset that Jacob had to flee for his life to another country. He lived for nearly twenty years with his uncle Laban. God blessed Jacob in great ways. He said to God, "I'm not worthy of all the faithfulness and unfailing love that You have shown me. I left home with only a walking stick, and now my household fills two camps." In spite of Jacob's past deceptions, God had blessed him with a large family, promoted him, and given him great wealth. Jacob recognized it was God's goodness.

Finally, Jacob decided to move back home and sent word to Esau that he was coming and that he hoped Esau would be friendly to him and his family. You can imagine how nervous Jacob was. He was about to see this brother whom he had taken advantage of and wronged. He didn't know if Esau was still angry and would seek revenge. It was a huge chance. So Jacob prayed, "God, please rescue me from my brother. I'm afraid that he's going to kill me and all my wives and children." He could have stopped there and just prayed the problem, but he understood this principle. He said, "But, God, You promised to treat me kindly and multiply my descendants." After all the bad choices, after all the manipulation and greed, what did Jacob do? He went back to a promise that God had made to him as a young man, and he said, "God, You promised to be good to me. You promised You would increase me." He met with Esau, and Esau not only forgave him but was very kind to him and welcomed him home.

What would happen if we had this same boldness as Jacob? What if in spite of the mistakes we've made and the times we've gotten off course, instead of living down on ourselves and giving up on our dreams, we would say, "God, You promised to be good to me. You promised to restore what the enemy has stolen. You promised to forgive me and not remember my mistakes." Put God in remembrance of what He promised—not what you think you deserve. Psalm 86 says, "God is merciful and compassionate, slow to anger and abounding in kindness and faithfulness." You

> *Put God in remembrance of what He promised— not what you think you deserve.*

have the promise that God made to Jacob. "God, You promised to be kind to me. You promised me a future filled with purpose and fulfillment." God is not holding your mistakes against you. Don't go through life holding them against yourself.

LIFE-CHANGING POWER

When Moses was leading two million Israelites through the desert to the Promised Land, God told him to go up on Mount Sinai, which is where he received the Ten Commandments. He left his brother, Aaron, in charge while he was on the mountain for forty days. The people got restless and said to Aaron, "We don't know if Moses is ever coming back. Let's make some gods out of gold that we can worship." Aaron had them melt down their earrings and jewelry, and he molded a calf out of the gold. Then they started partying, drinking, and committing all kinds of debauchery. God was so angry with Aaron and the people that He was going to wipe them all out and only spare Moses.

But in Exodus 32, it says, "Moses pleaded with the Lord, saying, 'Remember what You promised, that the descendants of Abraham, Isaac, and Jacob would be as numerous as the stars in the heavens, and that they would possess this land forever.'" Then it says, "God changed His mind and did not bring the disaster that He had threatened." That's how powerful it is when you remind God of what He promised. If Moses had not said, "God, You promised," He would have wiped them all out. I wonder if there are blessings, favor, healing, and vindication that we're not seeing because we're not putting God in remembrance of His promises. We're praying for Him to do it, we're asking Him to turn it around, which is good, but when you say, "God,

> When you say, "God, You promised," something powerful happens. The Creator of the universe goes to work.

You promised," something powerful happens. The Creator of the universe goes to work. Chains are broken, forces of darkness are pushed back, and impossible situations turn around. Nothing can stand against our God.

God says in Genesis 28, "I will be with you constantly until I have finished giving you everything I promised." God is saying, "Everything I've promised you is on the way. Healing is on the way. Promotion, freedom, opportunities, the right connections, and vindication are on the way." Get ready for God to show out in your life. I believe and declare that new doors are about to open, problems are turning around, and dreams are coming to pass.

CHAPTER FIVE

Kind Words Work Wonders

*The words you speak have the power to
nourish souls, soothe emotions, calm fears,
and bring healing and wholeness.*

When you say something kind, give a compliment, tell your spouse that you love them, or encourage your neighbor, it may seem like a simple thing, no big deal. But those words have incredible power. Proverbs 16 says, "Kind words are like honey—sweet to the soul and healthy for the body." You can make someone healthier by speaking kind words. It might just be a simple compliment: "You look beautiful today" or "You did great on that presentation." That's not just being nice, you're nourishing their soul. When you tell your spouse, "I love you. I'm so blessed to have you in my life," that's not only going to keep your relationship strong, but it's making your spouse more secure, more confident. It's nourishing them. When you call a friend who's down and say, "I'm thinking about you. I care about you. You mean the world to me," that's not just encouraging them, it's bringing healing to their body. Don't miss opportunities to bring nourishment. The people around you need what you have. Your kind words can be what pushes them into their destiny. Your encouragement and compliments are making them healthier and stronger. That's how they're going to become all they were created to be.

Maybe you weren't raised in a family that said nice things to one another, that gave compliments and said "I love you." You didn't see that modeled growing up. You can be the one to start it. Without your nourishing words, it will make it more difficult on your family, on your children. The reason some people aren't flourishing is that no one is nourishing them. They never hear any compliments, any encouragement. God created us to need one another. You have something that will cause your spouse to blossom, your children to bloom, your loved ones to feel more secure. It's not your money, your hard work, or your accomplishments; it's your kind words. They need to hear how much you love them, how much you believe in them, and how great you think they are. Don't let a day go by that you don't say something kind to the people God put in your life. It's not enough to

> *Don't let a day go by that you don't say something kind to the people God put in your life.*

just think it. Your thoughts don't nourish anyone. A blessing is not a blessing until it's spoken. They need to hear the blessing. "I love you. I'm proud of you. You're beautiful. You're going to do great things." Make it a habit of speaking kind words.

These days, nourishing words are needed more than ever. There are so many voices trying to push people down. So many people are saying harsh words, being rude, demeaning. They have no problem speaking their mind in a negative way. We need to be just as bold and speak our mind in a positive way. God is counting on us to be healers, to be lifters, to be encouragers. Let's make it our business to nourish people's souls, to bring healing and wholeness.

CALL OUT SEEDS OF GREATNESS

I've told Victoria how beautiful she is thousands of times. I realize she already knows that she's beautiful. People have been telling her that for her whole life. But do you know that she's never once said, "Joel, stop telling me I'm beautiful." Do you know why we like to hear good things over and over? Because it's nourishing our soul. It's keeping us strong and healthy. When I was growing up, my parents told me how proud they were of me again and again. Every night before bed, they would say, "Joel, we love you, and we're proud of you." Those words brought confidence and security. Because they believed in me, I believed in myself. There are people in your life who, when they know you believe in them, will start believing in themselves in a new way. They need your validation, your encouragement, your blessing. That's what will push them into their

> *There are people in your life who, when they know you believe in them, will start believing in themselves in a new way.*

destiny. This should start with your family. Don't take for granted the people who are closest to you. You may think, *They're strong. They don't need my blessing. They know I'm proud of them. They know they're beautiful.* No, something happens when they hear you say it. Those kind words get down into their spirit and bring a new level of confidence, talent, and boldness.

When I ran the television department at Lakewood, my father would bring guests by during the week. He would tell them, "You have to meet my son, Joel. He's so talented, and he's so much better looking than his brother, Paul. He can produce television like nobody else." He would brag on me so much that I'd be embarrassed. But Daddy knew the power of kind words. He didn't grow up with people encouraging him. He had loving parents, but they weren't vocal about their love. They expressed themselves when they saw something negative, something that displeased them. Yes, we have to correct our children, but they shouldn't only hear what they're doing wrong. They need to hear words of affirmation, how valuable they are, how much you love them. Talk to them about what they're good at. I may have acted as though I didn't like all those times when my father bragged on me, but the truth is, I did like it. It made me believe in myself in a greater way.

You have to call out the seeds of greatness in the

> *They need to hear words of affirmation, how valuable they are, how much you love them.*

people God put in your life. Most of the time, that greatness won't come out on its own. They have to hear it again and again. My mother recently sent me a birthday card that says, "Joel, I'm so proud of you, and I know Daddy would be so proud, too." Ninety years old and she's still speaking the blessing over her children. No wonder I've been able to go places I've never dreamed. I didn't think I could ever minister, but people around me kept calling it out, telling me what I could become. Their kind words nourished my soul, made me more confident, more secure, and helped me to step into my destiny.

WORDS THAT NOURISH THE SOUL

I wouldn't be half of who I am today without Victoria. She saw things in me that I couldn't see. Here's the key: She took time to tell me. She spoke words of faith, words of victory, not once but over and over. "Joel, you can do anything. You're amazing. You're so talented." Years ago, we bought an old house, had it torn down, and were going to build a new one. I called the builder who had built a previous house for us that we really liked. But Victoria said, "Why are you calling him? We don't need a builder. You can build the house." I answered, "Victoria, I am not a builder. I don't know how to build a house." She replied, "Sure you do. You just watched him build our last house. You're as smart as he is. You can build this house." I said, "Victoria, I had surgery on my knee. I watched the surgeon, but I can't do surgery." She responded, "That's different," then she proceeded to talk me into it. I built the house, and it turned out pretty well. I forgot the plumbing, but other than that it was great.

Ten years before my father went to be with the Lord, Victoria and I would sit in the front row when Daddy was at the pulpit ministering on Sunday nights. Victoria would lean over and say, "Joel, one day you're going to pastor the church." I thought, *I have her so fooled. I may be able to build a house, but I can't get up and speak in front of people.* I would tell her, "There's no way." She would respond, "Yes, I can see it. I know you can do it." When my father passed, one of the reasons I believe I was able to step up and pastor, even though I had never ministered, is that I had heard Victoria

> *How much further will the people who God put in your life go if you speak kind words to them?*

tell me I could do it hundreds of times. Those words nourished my soul, gave me confidence, and brought talent out that I hadn't known I had. How much further will the people who God put in your life go if you speak kind words to them? How much higher will they go if you tell them what they can become and call out their seeds of greatness? Thinking about it doesn't do them any good. Speak it over them.

Here's a key: Be generous with your compliments and be stingy with your complaints. It's easy to focus on things that we don't like about someone, how they don't measure up, how they should do better. Don't spend more time telling people what you don't like and what they can't do than you do telling them what you do like and what they can do. You have the power to push them into their destiny. Many times, you can see things in people that they can't see in themselves. Your kind words can be the seed that causes them to blossom. Because you spoke faith, because you encouraged, because you lifted them with your words, they'll step into levels that they couldn't get to on their own. There may be people in your life now with whom you're not happy. Why can't they be more disciplined? Why haven't they gone further? Maybe all they need is some nourishment. Maybe your encouragement and kind words will give them the strength, the confidence, and the faith to rise up and blossom into who they were created to be.

WORDS THAT BRING HEALING

We have this small plant in a pot on our back porch. We were out of town for a couple of weeks and didn't water it. When we came back, the plant was completely wilted and the leaves were dry and brown. It looked dead. I was going to take it to the trash, but Victoria said, "No, Joel, it's not dead. Just put some water in it." I thought, *Man, she has more faith than I do. There's nothing in this plant that looks alive.* I watered it, and the next morning the plant was standing up tall. I thought it was a miracle. This was a resurrection. Two days later, the leaves had turned green. A couple of weeks later, there were beautiful flowers. The whole plant was blossoming, blooming, prettier than ever. I thought it was dead when all it needed was some nourishment.

The reason some people are wilted, not blossoming, and not reaching their potential is that they're lacking nourishment. They need someone to speak life into them. You have what they need. If you encourage them, let them know that you believe in them, and call out their seeds of greatness, you'll see them come to life as the plant did. Gifts will come out that they hadn't known they had. Their passion will come back. Before long, they'll be blossoming, blooming, and stepping into new levels. It wasn't something they could do on their own. They needed what you have. Your kind words are nourishment to their soul.

> *The reason some people are wilted, not blossoming, and not reaching their potential is that they're lacking nourishment.*

This is not something that's complicated to do, and it doesn't take a lot of time. In twenty seconds, you can give someone a compliment. You can send someone a text that says, "I'm thinking about you. I appreciate your friendship. You're really amazing." You just nourished their soul. You just lightened their load, made their life a little easier. You don't know what people are going through. They may be smiling on the outside, everything seems fine, but they're hurting inside. They're trying to keep it together. Everyone is fighting a battle. Everyone is dealing with something. They may not show it, but they're carrying a heavy load. There are thoughts telling them how something is not going to work out. They may be concerned about a child, worried about their health, or struggling in their career. If they were sick and we had the medicine that would cure them, none of us would withhold it. We'd be quick to give it to them. We want to see them get better. What I'm saying is that we have some medicine. We have something that will not only nourish their soul, soothe their emotions, and calm their fears, but our kind words bring healing to the body. When you tell someone, "It's going to be okay. It's going to work out. God has you in the palms of His hands," that just made them stronger. Their immune system will function better, their cells will work more efficiently, and their blood pressure will improve. All because you took time to be a healer.

WORDS THAT IMPACT FOR A LIFETIME

The book of Proverbs says, "A word of encouragement works wonders." We often pray for signs and wonders, and I believe in that. But what if some of those wonders are in our kind words? What if the miracle is in something as simple as telling someone that they're going to make it? What if it comes through telling your spouse that you love them every day, or giving your coworker a compliment, or encouraging your

> *What if the miracle is in something as simple as telling someone that they're going to make it?*

friend? Don't discount the power of a kind word. When you speak the blessing, it can work wonders.

My mother had polio as a child, and it caused one of her legs to be much smaller than the other. She's always walked with a limp, which used to really bother her. She was self-conscious about it, thinking, *People are looking at me, thinking there's something wrong with me.* She would try to cover up her smaller leg with long dresses. One day a minister friend was speaking at our church. He and my father were walking together, and my mother was walking a few feet in front of them. The minister friend turned to my father and said, "John, look at Dodie. She walks like a princess." My mother had never heard anyone say anything positive about how she walked. But when she heard that, it changed her whole perspective. She stopped being embarrassed by it. She started walking with confidence, knowing that she's made in the image of Almighty God. That was over

> *One compliment, one kind word, can have an impact for a lifetime.*

forty years ago, but she remembers it as though it was yesterday. One compliment, one kind word, can have an impact for a lifetime.

What if that minister had just thought that thought but never said it? Maybe my mother would still be bothered by the way she walks. But a word of encouragement works wonders. Your kind words can break strongholds in people's minds. Your encouragement can set their dreams into motion. Don't withhold the healing. The plant on our porch that needed water couldn't water itself. I had to step in. Someone needs your water. God is counting on us to bring the nourishment. You don't know how a simple act of kindness can impact a person. It seems ordinary to us, but to that person, it's something that will affect them for the good for years to come.

IT'S IN YOUR POWER TO GIVE

When I first started ministering, I was so insecure. I hadn't been trained to minister, and I'm naturally quiet and reserved. All these thoughts told me, *Nobody is*

going to listen to you, Joel. It's a big mistake. You'd bet-
ter change your mind and go back to the television pro-
duction. I was fighting all these internal battles, trying
to keep moving forward, unsure of myself. After about
two months, when I was at a critical point, I received
a letter from a very well-known, well-respected minister and business leader. I had never met him, and I
didn't even know that he knew who I was. I was so
nervous when I started reading the letter, not knowing what to expect. But he said, "Joel, I want you to
know that I've been watching you, and I can't tell you
how great you're doing." He listed all the things I was
doing right, on and on, so encouraging, so uplifting.
When he sent that letter, he had no idea of what I
was fighting. He had no way of knowing what kind of
impact it would have. But he took the time to nourish my soul. He took the time to let me know that he
cared, that he was for me, that he believed in me. That
letter had a big part in helping me to move forward
and push through the doubt, the naysayers, and my
own negative thoughts.

In Proverbs 3, it says, "When it's in your power,
don't withhold the good." This has taught me to live

my life as a healer, to be free with kind words, to lift people up, to speak life into their dreams, to tell them what they can become. Several times a week when I'm at home, instead of watching television, I scroll through the contacts on my cell phone and think, *Who can I encourage? Who can I bless? Who can I nourish?* As that man did for me, I want to speak a word in due season to someone. There are people all around us—at work, at the grocery store, the mall, the gym—who need nourishment. Life has pushed them down. They're trying to decide as I was: "Should I give up on this dream?" It might be that they're about to give up on their marriage or their child. They're starting to wilt, to dry up. The good news is, you have the water. You have the nourishment. Your kind words, your spoken encouragement, or your compliment in a text can be what causes them to come back to life.

> *Your kind words, your spoken encouragement, or your compliment in a text can be what causes them to come back to life.*

"But, Joel, I need someone to nourish me. I have challenges.

I'm under a heavy load." The Scripture says, "Your own soul is nourished when you're kind." When you're kind to others, you're not only nourishing them, but you're being nourished. You're going to get stronger, you're going to get healthier, you're going to have more favor.

HELP PUT PEOPLE BACK ON THEIR FEET

The prophet Isaiah says, "Say to the righteous that all will be well with them." He didn't say to pray for the righteous, although that's good. He didn't say to tell the righteous how to get out of their problem. He simply says, "Say to the righteous that it's going to work out. Everything's going to be okay." Just say a word of encouragement. Just let them know that you care. Remind them that God is still on the throne. You don't have to have all the answers. I used to be intimidated when someone's situation was so complicated and I wasn't sure what to tell them. Perhaps several people were involved and there had been a loss. I've learned, though, that I don't have to solve the problem; that's God's job. My part is to just nourish their soul and say, "I care about you. I'm standing with you. You're going to make it." Those kind words are what put people back on their feet.

Years ago, a minister friend of mine went through a tough time. He was publicly accused of doing things that were wrong. People blew them way out of proportion, made it a really big deal, and his ministry and reputation went down to nothing. He's a good man, but he made some mistakes, got a little off course. It's easy to be judgmental and say, "He knew better. It's his own fault. He's getting what he deserves." But a true friend doesn't run away when people are in trouble; a friend runs to them. You pour oil on their wounds. You help them get better. They have enough people pushing them down. Their own thoughts are making them feel badly enough. Why don't you be a healer? Why don't you use your words to nourish their soul? You

> *A true friend doesn't run away when people are in trouble; a friend runs to them.*

I couldn't tell if it made any difference, but at least he knew that we cared.

Two months later, he called and told me that at the time of our call, he had already made up his mind to get out of the ministry. He was going to formally resign and do something else. But he said, "When I heard your voice that day, something came alive inside. I kept hearing what you told me, that God still has a purpose for me." He quit dwelling on his failures and quit listening to the accusing voices. He got his passion back. Today, he's back in the ministry, stronger than ever, making a greater difference than before.

On your journey in life, you're going to meet people like this who are wilted. Life has thrown them a curve. They feel overwhelmed, and people are judging them. God put them in your path so you can nourish them. Your kind words can help put them back on their feet. They don't need more judgment; they need a healer. They need someone who will pour oil on the wounds. There are a lot of tears in our world today. There is a lot of heartache, a lot of pain. When we get to Heaven, the Scripture says that God will wipe away the tears. There will be no more tears, no more loss, no

can help love them back into wholeness. The mer
we show others is the mercy God is going to sho
us. I don't want to be a condemner, a faultfinder,
"I told you so." I'm going to live my life as a heale
The Scripture says, "The enemy is the accuser of th
brethren." Anytime you're tempted to be harsh, judg
mental, and condemning, recognize that you're on th
wrong side.

After all the news hit about this minister, it was as
though the whole world turned against him. A few
months later, I called my friend on his cell phone.
He answered in the weakest, faintest voice you could
imagine. I could barely hear him say hello. He's a very
outgoing, dynamic person. I told him how much I
loved him, how this was not the end, and that God
knows how to restore. The call went silent when I
paused. I could tell he was weeping. He said, "Joel, I
don't have any fight left in me." I said, "That's okay.
We're going to fight for you." I didn't have the solution, and I didn't know how it was going to work out.
But I let him know that God still had a purpose for
him, that he was not finished, and we were going to
keep praying for him. It was a five-minute phone call.

more pain. But while we're here on Earth, God is counting on us to wipe away the tears, to lift the fallen, to

> *God is counting on us to wipe away the tears, to lift the fallen, to nourish the wilted, to encourage those who are down.*

nourish the wilted, to encourage those who are down. Your kind words can breathe life back into their spirits. Your nourishing words can set their dreams into motion. Your encouragement can be what causes them to step into their purpose.

KEEP SINGING, KEEP ENCOURAGING

I read about a three-year-old boy named Michael whose mother had found out she was pregnant with a little girl. Michael was so excited and couldn't wait to see his little sister. All through the day, he would come over to his mother's tummy and sing to his baby sister, "You are my sunshine, my only sunshine." Week after week, month after month, hundreds of times, he sang to his sister. When his mother finally went into labor, there were complications with the delivery. She had to be rushed to the operating room for an emergency C-section. Unfortunately, the baby didn't fare well. She was alive, but the doctors told the parents there was very little chance she would survive. The baby was taken to the neonatal intensive care unit. All the while, Michael kept asking, "When can I see my baby sister?" Several days went by, then word came that the baby probably would not make it through the night. The mother knew that if Michael didn't see his sister right away, he might not ever see her alive.

When the head nurse wasn't watching, the mother snuck Michael into the intensive care unit. He was taken aback by all the tubes and monitors on his little sister. About that time, a nurse saw Michael and told the mother that he had to leave immediately. Without his mother saying a word, Michael started singing to his sister, "You are my sunshine, my only sunshine. You make me happy when skies are gray." The nurse noticed the baby's rapid breathing began to slow down to normal. She looked at little Michael and said, "Keep singing." As he stood there and sang for a few minutes, the nurse watched in amazement as his baby sister's heart rate became normal and her blue skin color began to fade away. Instead of being shaky and jittery, a calmness came over his sister. It was as though those words from a three-year-old brother were releasing healing and wholeness into his sister. Against all odds, she got better. Today, she's perfectly healthy and whole. Kind words work wonders.

Are you using your healing powers? Are you nourishing anyone's soul? Don't let the day go by without encouraging someone, giving a compliment, telling your family that you love them. Develop the habit of speaking kind words. The Scripture says, "Encourage one another daily." This is not a onetime thing and you're done; this should be a lifestyle. Be on the lookout for who you can encourage today, who you can text, who you can call. There

> *Are you using your healing powers? Are you nourishing anyone's soul?*

are people God has put in your path that need your nourishment. Remember, when you're kind to others, your own soul is nourished. If you do this, I believe and declare that as you help them, you're going to rise higher. New doors are going to open, healing will come, favor, breakthroughs, and abundance.

CHAPTER SIX

Your Words Become Your Reality

When you speak blessing, faith, favor, and victory, that's what allows God to do the impossible.

You are where you are today in part because of what you've been saying about yourself. Words are like seeds. When you speak something out, you give life to what you're saying. If you continue to say it, eventually that can become a reality. Whether you realize it or not, you are prophesying your future. This is great when you're making statements such as, "I'm blessed. I'm strong. I will accomplish my dreams. I'm coming out of debt." That's not just being positive, that's prophesying victory, prophesying success, prophesying new levels. Your life will move in the direction of your words. But too many people go around prophesying the opposite. "I never get any good breaks." "I'll never get back in shape." "Business is slow. I'll probably get laid off." "Flu season is here. I always get it." They don't realize they are prophesying defeat. It's just as though they're calling in bad breaks, mediocrity, and lack.

> *Words are like seeds. When you speak something out, you give life to what you're saying.*

In a previous chapter, we read that the Scripture says, "We will eat the fruit of our words." You are planting seeds when you talk. At some point, you're going to eat the fruit. My challenge is that you make sure you're planting the right kind of seeds. If you want apples, you have to sow apple seeds. If you want oranges, you can't plant cactus seeds, poison ivy seeds, or mushroom seeds. You're going to reap fruit from the exact seeds that you've been sowing. In other words, you can't talk negative

> *You're going to reap fruit from the exact seeds that you've been sowing.*

and expect to live a positive life. You can't talk defeat and expect to have victory. You can't talk lack, not enough, can't afford it, or never get ahead and expect to have abundance. If you have a poor mouth, you're going to have a poor life. If you don't like what you're seeing, start sowing some different seeds.

Instead of saying, "I'll never get well. This sickness has been in my family for three generations," you need to be planting the right seeds by saying, "God is restoring health to me. This sickness didn't come to stay, it came to pass. I'm getting better and better every day." You keep sowing those seeds, and eventually you'll eat that fruit—health, wholeness, victory. Instead of saying, "I'll never get out of debt. I'll never rise any higher," you need to say, "I will lend and not borrow. Whatever I touch prospers and succeeds. I'm coming into overflow, into more than enough." Start sowing seeds of increase, seeds of abundance. No more saying, "I'll never accomplish my dreams." Turn it around and say, "I have the favor of God. Blessings are chasing me down. The right people are searching me out. New opportunities and new levels are in my future." If you keep talking like that, you'll reap a harvest of good things.

START BLESSING YOUR LIFE

James says in the Scripture, "With our tongue we can bless our life or we can curse our life." Many people don't realize that

> *Many people don't realize that they're cursing their future with their words.*

they're cursing their future with their words. Every time you say, "I never get any good breaks," you just cursed your life. "I'll never be able to afford that nice house." "I'll never be able to break this addiction." "I'll never meet the right person." No, stop cursing your future. Sometimes the enemy doesn't have to defeat us; we defeat ourselves. Pay attention to what you're saying. Are you blessing your life, or are you cursing it?

I had a classmate in high school who was always very negative. Every time I asked him what was going on, he had this standard answer: "Not much. I'm just getting old, fat, and bald." I heard him say that probably five hundred times. I know he was just kidding, but I wouldn't kid about that. He was one of the stars on our football team, always in great shape, and he had thick curly hair. About fifteen years later, I ran into him at the mall. When I saw him, I nearly passed out. He had prophesied his future. He looked old, way overweight, and bald. Don't speak that defeat over your life. Our attitude should be: *I'm getting younger. God is renewing my youth like an eagle. I'm getting stronger, healthier, and better looking. I'm going to keep my hair. I'm going to stay in my right mind. I'm going to live a long and productive faith-filled life.*

Don't go around cursing your future. Start blessing your life. Prophesy good things. There's a young lady on our church staff who really knows how to do this. Every morning before she leaves the house, she looks in the mirror and says, "Girl, you're looking good today." I saw her one time and asked if she was still doing it. She said, "Yes, in fact, today when I looked in the mirror, I said, 'Girl, some days you look good. But today, you look *really* good.'"

Why don't you stop criticizing yourself? Why don't you stop talking about all the things you don't like about yourself—how you're getting too old, too wrinkled, too this, too that? Stop cursing your life and start blessing your life. Start calling yourself strong, healthy, talented, beautiful, and young. Every morning before you leave

> *Why don't you stop talking about all the things you don't like about yourself—how you're getting too old, too wrinkled, too this, too that?*

the house, look in the mirror and say, "Good morning, you good-looking thing." My brother, Paul, needs to do this every hour.

Sometimes after we've been traveling a lot or been very busy, Victoria will come to church with me and say, "Joel, I am so tired. Look at me. Can you see how red my eyes are?" I always answer, "No, Victoria, you look beautiful. You look as great as ever." She responds, "No, I don't, Joel. I know you just won't tell me." She's right. I don't want to speak defeat. I want to speak victory over her life. I wonder what she would do if I ever said, "Yes, you're right. You don't look good at all." I'm smarter than that.

I know a man who was so concerned that he was going to get Alzheimer's disease. Several people in his family had it, including his grandfather and a great uncle. This man was only in his early fifties, but he was always talking about what might happen. He told me that he was making plans for who would take care of him, getting everything lined up. Of course, it's good to use common sense, to be wise and make plans for your life. But if you go around talking about when you're going to get a disease and making plans for it, you probably won't be disappointed. You're calling it in. It's just as though you're sending it an invitation. I told him what I'm telling you: "Don't say another word about getting that disease. Start declaring, 'No weapon formed against me will ever prosper. I will live out my days in good health, with a clear mind, with a good memory, with clarity of thought. My mind is alert. My senses are sharp. My youth is being renewed.'" You have to prophesy health. Prophesy a long productive life. Your words will become your reality.

When our daughter, Alexandra, was four years old, she overheard Victoria and me talking about a little boy whose headaches were so bad that he was having to leave school and was experiencing all kinds of difficulties. Alexandra spoke up and said, "Daddy, I don't have headaches, and I never will have headaches." I thought, *You're exactly right. You're prophesying the right thing.* On another occasion, I didn't realize Alexandra was standing behind me when I was working on my garage door. I couldn't get the door to go up, and I was getting frustrated. When I said, "This thing is never going to work," I heard this little voice speak up:

"Daddy, you're going to have what you say."

"Daddy, you're going to have what you say." I thought, *It's terrible when your own children believe your messages.*

DON'T GET TRAPPED BY YOUR WORDS

In Proverbs 6, it says, "We are snared by the words of our mouth." *Snared* means "to be trapped." Your words can trap you. What you say can cause you to stumble. It can keep you from your potential. You're not snared by what you think. Negative thoughts come to us all. But when you speak them out, you give them life. That's when they become a reality. When you say, "I'll never get back in shape," it becomes more difficult. You just made it harder. When you say, "I never get any good breaks," that stops the favor that was ordained for you. If you say, "I'm not that talented. I don't have a good personality," that is setting the limits for your life. That is calling in mediocrity.

You may have been snared in the past, trapped by your words, but this is a new day. I declare that you're coming out of that trap. Every chain is being loosed. Every stronghold is coming down. No weapon formed against you is going to prosper. Now you have to do your part. Start speaking the blessing over your life. Speak increase. Dare to declare God's favor. Be bold to call in those things that you're dreaming about, those things that you're believing for. Don't use your words to describe the situation; use your words to change the situation.

In Matthew 6, Jesus was talking about worry. He said, "Take no thought for your life, saying, 'What shall we eat? What shall we drink?'" Notice the phrase *take no thought, saying.* The negative thoughts will come. The key is to not say them. A thought will die stillborn if you don't speak it. Jesus was saying, "You may feel worried. It may seem as though it's never going to happen. But take no thought saying. Don't verbalize it. Don't get trapped by your words."

> *The negative thoughts will come. The key is to not say them.*

When we acquired the former Compaq Center for our church facility, it was a dream come true. We were so excited. Our builders drew up plans to renovate it from a professional basketball arena to a church, then they called us together and said it was going to cost a hundred million dollars. After they picked me up off the floor, my first thoughts were, *That's impossible. There's no way. I've only been the pastor four years. They cannot expect me to raise those kinds of funds.* Even though those thoughts were racing through my mind again and again, I knew I had to keep my mouth closed. I kept a big smile on my face, acted as though it was no big deal. I knew that if I didn't verbalize those negative thoughts, eventually they would die stillborn. It's one thing to think that it's impossible, but when you start telling people it's impossible, it takes on a whole new meaning.

You may think, *I'll never break this illness. I'll never get well. I'll never meet the right person. I'll never have the finances for this.* Those thoughts come to all of us. You can't stop that. My challenge is, don't give them life by speaking them out. Don't go call your friends and tell them how it's not going to happen. I told our team, "I don't see a way, but I know God has a way. He didn't bring us this far to leave us." My report was: "God is supplying all our needs. The funds are coming in. It may look impossible on paper, but with God all things are possible." I knew better than to curse my future. I didn't want to get trapped by my words. I knew if I kept prophesying the right things—increase, favor, more than enough—we would start moving toward it.

Especially during tough times, you have to be on guard. It's tempting to vent your frustration and tell people how the loan didn't go through, how bad the medical report was, how people aren't treating you right. But to continually talk about the problem will not only make you more discouraged, it will give the problem more life.

> *To continually talk about the problem will not only make you more discouraged, it will give the problem more life.*

You're making it bigger. Turn it around. Don't talk about the problem, talk about the promise. Instead of saying, "Oh, man, I have big challenges," you need to say, "I serve a big God. He spoke worlds into existence. Nothing's too difficult for Him." Instead of saying, "I didn't get the promotion. I was passed over again. Another big disappointment," you need to say, "I know when one door closes, God has something better. He's directing my steps. I'm excited about my future." Instead of saying, "I'll never meet the right person. I'm too old. It's been too long," you need to say, "Something good is going to happen to me. Divine connections are coming my way." If someone says to you, "I heard you received a bad medical report?" just say, "Yes, that's true. But I have another report. It says, 'God is restoring health to me.'" If someone else says, "Well, I heard those people did you wrong," you can respond, "Yes, but I'm not worried. God is my vindicator. He's fighting my battles. He's promised to give me beauty for ashes."

CHOOSE THE VOICE OF FAITH

In life, there are always two voices vying for your attention—the voice of faith and the voice of defeat.

You'll hear a voice saying, "The problem's too big. It's not going to work out. Just accept it." You'll be tempted to worry,

> *In life, there are always two voices vying for your attention—the voice of faith and the voice of defeat.*

to be negative, to complain. But if you listen carefully, you'll hear the voice of faith saying, "God has a way. Favor is coming. Healing is coming. Breakthroughs are coming." One voice will say, "You've reached your limits. You've gone as far as you can. You don't have what it takes." The other voice says, "You are well able. You can do all things through Christ. Your best days are still in front of you." Now, here's the deal. You get to choose which voice comes to life. The way you do it is by what you speak. When you verbalize that thought, you're giving it the right to come to pass. If you go around saying, "Oh, the problem's too big. I'll never get well," you are agreeing with the wrong voice. You have to get in agreement with God. The other voice may seem louder, but you can override it. You can take away all its power by choosing the voice of faith.

If you're going to a job interview, one voice will tell you, "You're not going to get it. You're wasting your time. These people are not going to like you." The other voice will say, "You have the favor of God. You're blessed. You're confident. You have what it takes." There's no use in going to that interview if you tell your spouse, "I don't think I'm going to get this job. They're not going to like me. I'm not qualified." You're being trapped by your words. You have to dig your heels in and say, "I am not giving life to any more defeat. I am not speaking lack. I'm not speaking sickness. I'm not speaking mediocrity, not enough. I'm going to choose the voice of faith. It says, 'I'm strong. I'm healthy. I'm blessed. I'm favored. I am a victor and not a victim.'"

In Chapter One, we saw what David did when he faced Goliath. It looked impossible. All the odds were against him. Goliath was a giant from Gath, a veteran warrior, the champion of the Philistine army. David was a shepherd with a sling, not even a sword, and only a teenager. If he had verbalized his negative thoughts, that would have kept him from his destiny. Even though he had been anointed by Samuel to be the next king, those negative words would have kept him trapped in the shepherds' fields. He could have easily gone around saying,

Even though he had been anointed by Samuel to be the next king, those negative words would have kept him trapped in the shepherds' fields.

"Well, someone needs to go out and defeat Goliath, but as much as I want to be the one, it's not going to be me. I value my life too much to face him." You can talk yourself out of your destiny. Negative words can keep you from becoming who you were created to be. Don't fall into that trap. Quit calling in defeat. Quit talking about how it's not going to happen. You can pray in faith, ask God to turn it around, to do the impossible. That's good, but if you then walk away and start talking about how you're not going to get well or how your child's never going to straighten up, those negative words just canceled out that prayer.

"Joel, I'm having a financial crisis. I prayed and asked God to help me, but I don't see how it's going to happen." No, zip that up. "Father, You are Jehovah

Jireh, the Lord my provider. You've done it for me in the past, and I know You'll do it for me again in the future." Don't let your words trap you. Negative talk brings negative results. But when you speak faith, favor, and victory, that's what allows God to do the impossible. David went out and stood before Goliath. He looked the giant in the eyes and said, "You come against me with a sword, with a spear, and with a javelin. But I come against you in the name of the Lord God of Israel. This day the Lord will deliver you into my hand, and I will strike you down." Notice that he was prophesying victory. He may have felt fear, but he spoke faith. As

> *He may have felt fear, but he spoke faith.*

David was going out to face Goliath, I can imagine him saying under his breath, "I am well able. I am anointed. I am equipped. If God be for me, who dare be against me?" He picked up that rock, put it in his sling and slung it. That rock brought Goliath tumbling down.

When you face giants in life, when you face

challenges, you have to do as David did and prophesy your future. Say to the cancer, "Cancer, you are no match for me. I will defeat you." "This addiction may have been in my family for years, but this is a new day. The buck stops with me. I'm the difference maker. I am free." "My child may have been off course for a long time, but I know it's only temporary. As for me and my house, we will serve the Lord." Prophesy victory over your life.

PROPHESY TO THE MOUNTAINS

There was a man in the Scripture named Zerubbabel who was in charge of the rebuilding of the temple at Jerusalem. He was facing a huge mountain, a big obstacle. But he had God's promise through the prophet Zechariah: "So, big mountain, who do you think you are? Next to Zerubbabel you're nothing but a molehill." As David had done, Zerubbabel didn't talk about how impossible it was, how it was never going to work out. I can hear him saying, "Who are you, great mountain, to stand before me? You shall become a

> *Don't talk about the mountain; talk to the mountain.*

mere molehill." Zerub-babel was prophesying his future. The mountain looked big, but he declared God's promise that it would be flattened out. There's the principle: Don't talk about the mountain; talk to the mountain.

Look at the mountain of debt and tell it, "You can't defeat me. You're coming down. I will lend and not borrow. My cup will run over." Whatever mountains you face in life, no matter how big they look, don't shrink back in fear, don't be intimidated. Rise up in faith and tell the mountain, "You're coming down." Tell the sickness, "You're temporary." Say to the loneliness, the addiction, or the legal problem, "Who are you, great mountain, to stand before me?" In other words, you're saying, "Don't you know who I am? I'm a child of the Most High God. Haven't you read my birth certificate? My Father created the universe. He breathed life into me. He crowned me with His favor. He calls me more than a conqueror. That means you can't defeat me. You can't hold me back, great mountain. You have to come down. I will overcome this illness. I will break this addiction. I will pay my house off. I will see my family restored. I will accomplish my dreams."

What am I saying? Prophesy victory. Prophesy breakthroughs. Prophesy what you're believing for. In the Old Testament, the prophet Ezekiel saw a vision. He had this dream

> *Prophesy victory. Prophesy breakthroughs. Prophesy what you're believing for.*

of a valley filled with bones from people who had died. Everywhere he looked, it was acres and acres of bones, like a huge graveyard. Bones represent things in our life that look dead, situations that seem impossible, problems that look like they'll never change. God told him to do something interesting. He said, "Ezekiel, prophesy to these dead bones. Say to them, 'O dry bones, hear the word of the Lord!'" In this vision, Ezekiel started speaking to the bones, telling them to come back to life. There was a rattling and then the bones started to come back together, just like in a movie. He called for tissue, muscle, and skin, and as he was speaking, the bodies began morphing back into people. Finally, God told him to prophesy "to the breath, and call it forth." The Scripture says, "As he prophesied, breath came into those bodies, and they lived, and stood upon their feet, an exceedingly great army."

You may have things in your life that seem dead. It's not enough to just pray about it; you need to speak to it. Prophesy to those dead bones. Call in health. Call in abundance. Call in restoration. Don't just pray about your child who's been off course. Prophesy and say, "Son, daughter, come back in. You will fulfill your destiny." If you're struggling with an addiction, don't just pray about it. Prophesy and say, "I am free. Chains are broken off me. This is a new day of victory." If your finances look like a pile of dead bones, prophesy and say, "Debt, lack, and struggle are ending. I will lend and not borrow. I am the head and not the tail. I am coming into overflow." If you do as Ezekiel did and prophesy to the bones, God will resurrect

> *If you do as Ezekiel did and prophesy to the bones, God will resurrect what looks dead.*

what looks dead. He'll make things happen that you could never make happen.

DECLARE A DECREE

Psalm 2 says, "I will declare a decree." A decree was something that was written down as an official document. The psalmist was saying, "There's something that's been written that I'm going to start speaking." You and I can do the same thing and declare a decree. You should write down your goals. Write down what you want to see happen in life. Write down any areas in which you're struggling, where you need to improve, and declare that it's already done. Then every day, declare that decree. Read over it out loud a couple of times. It's not enough to just think it. Something happens when we speak. You have to prophesy your future. You can personalize your decree, but let me give you some generic things that should be in yours: "I am strong. I am healthy. I am disciplined. I am in shape. I weigh what I'm supposed to weigh. I am full of energy. I am passionate. I am talented. I am secure.

I am valuable. I am confident. I have a good personality. People like me. I am fun to be around. I am happy. I enjoy my life. I am a person of excellence. I am full of integrity. I am successful. I am prosperous. My future is bright. My children are mighty in the land. My legacy will live on to inspire future generations. I run with purpose in every step. I am blessed. I am victorious. I am a child of the Most High God."

If you keep speaking declarations of blessing such as those over your life, those words will get down inside you. They'll not only change your outlook, but they will change who you are. Your words will become your reality. You are prophesying your future. And over time, those words will become a part of your everyday vocabulary. It will be no big deal for you to go around saying, "I'm blessed. I'm healthy. I have the favor of God." Instead of being trapped by your words, you'll be propelled by your words.

The Scripture says, "Just as a tiny rudder controls a large ship, so the tongue sets the direction for our life." Are you going in the right direction? Are you seeing increase, favor, and new growth? If not, check out what you're saying. When you get your words going in the right direction, your life will go in the right direction. Make this decision with me: No

> *Are you going in the right direction? Are you seeing increase, favor, and new growth?*

more words of lack, defeat, can't do it, mediocrity, or doubt. Don't curse your future; bless your future. If you start prophesying victory, prophesying favor, I believe and declare that you're going to rise higher, overcome every obstacle that looks insurmountable, and accomplish dreams that seem impossible.

CHAPTER SEVEN

An Atmosphere of Praise

When you're always thanking God for who He is and what He's done, you're going to draw in favor, good breaks, peace, and joy.

We are all creating an atmosphere around us by what we're thinking, by what we're saying, and by our attitudes. It's easy to go around being negative. "Look at this doctor's report. The traffic is so bad. These people did me wrong." Whatever you're sending out, you're going to draw in. If you're creating a negative atmosphere, that's going to attract discouragement, defeat, and bad breaks. But when you create an atmosphere of praise, when you're always thanking God for what He's done, you get up in the morning and say, "Lord, thank You that I'm alive today. Thank You for my beautiful children. Thank You that goodness and mercy are following me. Thank You that I'm surrounded by Your favor. Thank You that You've made me invisible to the enemy." That faith-filled atmosphere is going to draw in favor, good breaks, peace, and joy. Pay attention to what kind of atmosphere you're creating. You can't complain and expect to see breakthroughs. You can't go around talking about problems, about how it's not going to work out, about a challenge being too big, and reach your potential. That negative atmosphere is stopping your victory.

The Scripture says, "God inhabits the praises of His people." He doesn't inhabit complaints, worry, or frustration. "Why is this taking so long? These children are getting on my nerves." That doesn't get God's attention. But when He hears you talking about His greatness, praising Him when you could be complaining, declaring His promises when you're up against giants, thanking Him that He's working when nothing is changing, that's when God says, "Let Me step in. Let Me fight that battle. Let Me make a way. Let Me bring promotion, healing, and favor." Other translations of that scripture say, "God is enthroned on our praises." When you're full of praise, you're building a throne for God to sit on.

> *When you're full of praise, you're building a throne for God to sit on.*

When you go through the day grateful, focused on what's right, with a spring in your step, with a smile on your face, and being good to people, that's not just having a good attitude. You're inviting God into your life, into your circumstances, into your emotions.

When you're up against challenges that seem too

big, dreams that look impossible, you'll be tempted to worry, live stressed, and complain. But the best thing you can do is give God praise. A challenge may be too much for you, but it's not too much for Him. David says, "Magnify the Lord with me." Don't magnify your problem, magnify your God. Thank Him for who He is. "Lord, thank You that You are the all-powerful Creator of the universe. Thank You that You are the Great I Am. You are my provider, my healer, my protector, my deliverer, my way maker." That's what causes God to show up. It's not begging Him and saying, "God, You have to do something." It's not complaining, "God, it's not fair." It's not worrying and thinking, *What am I going to do?* That's attracting the wrong things. Switch over into praise. That's what attracts the most powerful force in the universe.

PRAISE HAS A SWEET-SMELLING AROMA

Victoria and I were at a huge nursery and garden center recently, with several acres of various plants, flowers, and shrubs. We had been going up and down the rows for half an hour when we came to a section of a particular flower that had hundreds of bees around it. There were bees everywhere you looked. It had so many bees on it that you could barely see the individual flowers. I asked the garden specialist who was working there why this flower had so many bees while the ones right next to it had none. He told us that this flower puts off a sweet smell that attracts the bees. We saw hundreds of other types of flowers that day, row after row, but this was the only flower with bees on it. There were other flowers that even looked like this flower. They were just as beautiful and colorful. They had their own odors, but they didn't have any bees. The bees were looking for this specific sweet smell of nectar, so they passed over all the other flowers until they came to this flower.

The Scripture says that our praise goes up as a sweet-smelling aroma before God. When you give God praise, you're putting off the aroma that attracts God. He can smell praise. He'll pass over person after person after person, then He comes to you and smells that sweet-smelling aroma. He hears you thanking

Him, going around grateful, talking about how blessed you are, speaking the blessing, and declaring His promises. "This is another day the Lord has made. I'm going to rejoice. I'm going to live this day happy. Father, thank You that as for me and my house, we're going to serve the Lord. Yes, I have some challenges, but I know that You being for me is more than the world being against me." I can imagine God saying to the angels, "I smell something good. Do you smell it? There's a sweet-smelling aroma coming up. I'm going to go and find who it's coming from." Your praise will attract God. He will pass over all the other people and find the praiser. He'll find the one who has a report of victory, the one who's talking about how big their God is, not how big their problem is.

I wonder if what you're putting off is attracting God or causing Him to pass by. "Joel, this inflation is so bad. My back has been hurting. My coworkers are getting on my nerves. I can't stand driving in this traffic."

> *I wonder if what you're putting off is attracting God or causing Him to pass by.*

Instead of a sweet-smelling aroma, that's putting out a bad odor. That attitude stinks. I can hear God saying to the angels, "Go get me some air fresheners. Pick up some Odor-Eaters." That stench pushes God away. After we've been with some people for fifteen minutes, we can tell that they're bitter, they're a worrier, they're a complainer, they're jealous. Instead of a sweet-smelling aroma, instead of being grateful, joyful, and good-natured, they're putting out an unpleasant odor. Their attitude is sour. Their words are negative. They're focused on what's wrong, expecting the worst. Don't let what you're putting out keep you from your potential. Other people can't stop you. The enemy can't stop you. The only one that can stop you is you.

> *Other people can't stop you. The enemy can't stop you. The only one that can stop you is you.*

If you live negative, bitter, jealous, worried, and angry, none of those things attract God. You need God to reach the fullness of your destiny. You can't do it on your own. When you create an atmosphere of praise, you're going to attract favor, the right people, healing, freedom, and abundance.

It's interesting how our sense of smell works. We had an animal that died somewhere behind our backyard fence. It may have been a raccoon or squirrel. But the smell was so bad, the stench so strong, that I didn't want to go out in the yard. I tried to eat out on the back porch, but the smell was so powerful, so offensive, that it drove me away. At the same time, Victoria had baked a homemade chocolate cake, right out of the box. When I walked in the back door from the garage, which is two rooms away from the kitchen, I could smell the amazing aroma of that cake. She didn't have to tell me she had made the cake. She didn't have to announce, "Joel, I baked something for you." My nose knew exactly what she'd done. That smell drew me to it. I couldn't help it. I was attracted to it. That's how powerful our sense of smell is. I was pushed away from the stench in the backyard, and I was drawn to the sweet-smelling chocolate cake in the oven.

What is your life putting off? What is your attitude putting off? What are your words putting off? Sweet-smelling aromas? Or are you creating offensive odors, stinky attitudes, negative talk, living worried all the time. That's pushing God away. If you want to attract

> *What is your life putting off? What is your attitude putting off? What are your words putting off?*

favor, joy, peace, and creativity, start sending up some praise. Start thanking God for what He's done. Start bragging on His goodness. Start declaring victory over your life. You can't just be neutral and think, *Well, I'm not going to be negative. I'm not going to complain.* It's good that you're not putting out bad odors, but you need to send up some sweet-smelling aromas. "Lord, thank You for waking me up this morning. Thank You for giving me breath to breathe. Thank You that I'm healthy. Thank You for my family, for opportunities, for protection, for favor." That's creating an atmosphere of praise. That's what attracts the Most High God.

THE MELODY IN YOUR HEART

The Scripture talks about "singing and making melody in your heart to the Lord." We're all making

something. Some people are making sad songs, thinking about what went wrong, what wasn't fair, who
they lost. That's drawing in more sadness, more discouragement. Other people are making worry, playing all their negative thoughts over and over. *What if
it doesn't work out? What if I don't get well? I'll never
get past this problem.* That's drawing in more stress,
more heaviness. Why
don't you start mak-
ing melody, start hav-
ing a song of praise in
your heart? Instead of
saying, "These children
are so much trouble,"

> *Why don't you start
> making melody,
> start having a song
> of praise in your
> heart?*

make a melody and say, "Lord, thank You for blessing me with children." Instead of saying, "It's a pain
to go to work," turn it around and say, "Lord, thank
You that I have a job." Instead of saying, "Business is
slow. I'll never get ahead," let your melody be, "Lord,
thank You that You are my provider. Thank You that
You make streams in the desert." Instead of complaining, "The medical report is not good. I don't think
I'll ever get well," you need to say, "Lord, thank You

that You're restoring health to me." Are you sending up bad odors or fragrant aromas? Are you creating an atmosphere of doubt, worry, and mediocrity or an atmosphere of praise, an atmosphere of victory, an atmosphere of abundance?

I watched a funny YouTube video in which a man was dressed up as a bush, with green branches of leaves completely covering his face and body. As he crouched on a busy sidewalk, the people walking by thought it was just a bush until he stood up and scared them. It was all just for fun. When he stood up, the first thing about half the people did was let out a curse word. It just came out without them even thinking about it. The Scripture says, "Out of the heart, the mouth speaks." Whatever is in you is going to eventually come out of your mouth, especially when you're under pressure. Instead of cursing, the first thing about 10 percent of the people who were scared did was scream "Jesus." In the same situation, one is cursing and one is praising. What's the difference? It depends on what you're full of. You're going to be full of either doubt, worry, bitterness, and complaints or full of praise, thanksgiving, hope, faith, and victory. I want us to

be so filled with
praise that even
in unexpected
difficulties, the
first thing we
do is call on
the name of the

> *I want us to be so filled with praise that even in unexpected difficulties, the first thing we do is call on the name of the Lord.*

Lord. I want us to be declaring His goodness, talking about how great He is.

In my early twenties, I was driving home from work on the freeway in a really hard rain. When I went to change lanes, I hit a big pool of water and lost control of my car. I started spinning around and crossed three lanes of traffic. I hit the inside of the concrete barrier, which catapulted me and I started spinning back across the lanes. I looked up at one point and an eighteen-wheeler was right in front of me. I was facing the wrong direction; it was as if I could reach out and touch his front grille. I didn't have time to pray. I didn't have time to think about it. But I heard myself say, "Jesus! Jesus! Jesus!" Those words just came out of my mouth. The next thing I knew, I was stopped on the shoulder of the freeway. Somehow that big truck missed me. The truck driver pulled over, walked back to my car and up to my window. The first thing he said was, "Boy, you must be living right because right when I braced to hit you, a big gust of wind blew my truck into the other lane." I'm so glad I said "Jesus" and not blankety-blank. If I had said something else, I might not be here. When you stay full of praise, it will come out when you need it.

PRAISE SETS MIRACLES IN MOTION

In the Scripture, God told Jonah to go to the enemy city of Nineveh and tell them to repent, but Jonah didn't want to go. Instead, he got on a ship and headed in the opposite direction. The ship encountered a huge storm, and the crew thought they were all going to die. Jonah finally admitted that he was the problem. They said, "Thank you for telling us," then they threw him overboard. It should have been the end, but God in His mercy had a big fish waiting for Jonah that swallowed him. Jonah found himself in the belly of this fish. You can imagine how it stunk inside the fish's digestive system, with the gasses, fluids, and partially digested foods. It would have reeked and been almost unbearable. In Jonah 2,

> *Complaining and sending up stinky odors doesn't get God's attention.*

Jonah talked for eight verses about how bad his life was, how he was in the depths of despair, how he was surrounded by vast waters, how he didn't see a way out. All that was true, but complaining and sending up stinky odors doesn't get God's attention. "God, this isn't fair. Why did this happen? People did me wrong." That doesn't cause God to respond. What attracts Him are sweet-smelling aromas.

You may be in a stinky situation. As Jonah did, you can describe everything that's wrong, how you weren't treated right, how you're never going to get well. That's creating an atmosphere of doubt, defeat, and negativity. That's going to keep you where you are. After complaining for eight verses, Jonah had a change of heart. He must have tuned in to a live stream service from Lakewood. He said, "God, in spite of my difficulties, I'm going to offer the sacrifice of praise with the voice of thanksgiving." In the stomach of the fish, he started saying, "Lord, thank You that You're still in control. Thank You that Your mercy is bigger than my mistakes. Thank You that You didn't bring me this far to leave me, that what You started in my life, You will finish." I can hear God saying, "I smell a fragrant aroma coming from inside a fish. It should be stinky, it should be an offensive odor, but it's a sweet-smelling aroma. It's a song of praise. It's a song of victory."

The next verse says, "God commanded the fish, and it spit Jonah out onto the shore." When you praise in the midst of the trouble, when you talk about God's goodness when you don't see how it can work out, when you send up sweet-smelling aromas even though you're surrounded by

> *When you praise in the midst of the trouble, when you talk about God's goodness when you don't see how it can work out, when you send up sweet-smelling aromas even though you're surrounded by things that stink, that's when the Most High God will go to work.*

things that stink, that's when the Most High God will go to work. If God will cause a fish to take Jonah to the shore so he can fulfill his destiny, even after he disobeyed, God will cause your child to get back on course. God will cause the medical report to turn around. God will cause you to break the addiction, meet the right person, or have the baby. The question is, What are you sending up? Complaints, doubts, and worry? No, be a Jonah. In the middle of the stink, in the middle of the challenge, send up an aroma of praise. Send up faith, send up hope. "Lord, thank You that there's nothing too hard for You. Thank You that what You have purposed for my life will come to pass. Thank You that no person, no bad break, no sickness, no addiction, not even all the forces of darkness can stop Your plan."

The psalmist says, "Praise Him for His unequalled greatness. Praise Him for His mighty works. Praise Him for His majestic power." You may be limited, but He is unlimited. We're natural, but He's supernatural. When you don't see a way out, you'll be tempted to complain. No, turn it around and praise Him for who He is. "Lord, I praise You that You are bigger than this sickness. Praise You that You are stronger than this addiction. Praise You that You are greater than this trouble. Praise You that You are more powerful than these people." You could be sending up doubt, defeat, and complaints, but you're sending up sweet-smelling aromas, bragging on the goodness of God. Those fragrant aromas set miracles into motion. That's when God will show up and do what you cannot do.

DON'T HANG UP YOUR HARP

Sometimes we're waiting for our circumstances to change, then we'll give God praise, then we'll have a good attitude. But that's backward. You have to first give God praise. You have to have that song in your heart when nothing is changing. It seems as though

> *You have to first give God praise. You have to have that song in your heart when nothing is changing.*

it's never going to work out, but you're still thanking God that He's making ways where you don't see a way.

The Israelites had dwelt as a nation in the Promised Land for around eight hundred years before they were conquered and taken captive by the Babylonians. Their homes, lands, businesses, and freedoms were taken away, and they were forced to live and serve in a foreign land. Psalm 137 says, "They wept at the thought of Jerusalem." They were so discouraged, so disheartened. They used to be joyful. They used to talk about the greatness of Jehovah, how He had done amazing things. They had been filled with praise, but now they were in captivity; things hadn't worked out. They didn't just lose their freedom; they lost their praise and quit sending up the sweet-smelling aromas. It's easy to do when we're in difficult times. When life has thrown us a curve, we look back at what used to be and think about how great it was, how far we are from that. It's tempting to be negative, discouraged, and talk about how it used to be.

When the Israelites could have been thanking God that He was going to bring them back, they sat by the rivers of Babylon weeping, so discouraged over what they had lost. "They put away their harps and hung them on willow trees." Their captors asked them to sing the songs of Israel. They had heard about the joy, the dancing, the happy, uplifting songs. But the Israelites answered, "How can we sing the songs of the Lord while we're in a foreign land?" Their attitude was: *Once God delivers us, then we'll sing. Once I get well, once my child gets back on course, once this inflation goes down, then I'll get my joy back, then I'll go get my harp.* No, praise is what's going to cause it to turn around. While you're waiting for things to change, believing for breakthroughs, the enemy would love for you to hang up your harp. He would love for you to get discouraged, start complaining, and sit around and talk about your problems. No, that's when you need to give God praise more than ever. Praise activates His power. Praise causes angels to go to work. Praise opens prison doors. Praise breaks chains. Praise defeats giants.

> *Praise activates His power. Praise causes angels to go to work. Praise opens prison doors. Praise breaks chains. Praise defeats giants.*

Don't hang up your harp. You can praise your way out. If you start sending sweet-smelling aromas, you'll be amazed at what God will do.

When my mother was diagnosed with terminal cancer in 1981 and given a few weeks to live, she was tempted to hang up her harp. She'd been so healthy, so energetic. Now she weighed eighty-nine pounds and felt very sick. Like the Israelites, she didn't see a way out. That sickness had her in captivity. It looked as though that would be the end. But she didn't make the mistake that the Israelites made. She kept her harp. In the middle of that challenge, when every voice said she would never make it, when the doctors said it wasn't possible, she kept sending up praises. "Father, thank You that You can do the impossible. Thank You that the number of my days, You will fulfill. Thank You that I will live and not die and declare the works of the Lord." The more thoughts of defeat came against her mind, the more praises she sent up. You have to be more determined than the enemy. When the going gets tough, the tough have to get going. Maybe you need to get your harp back. Perhaps you've let a setback, a breakup, or a loss not just steal your joy but take your praise. You're wondering when

God is going to do something, but God is waiting for you to send up some fragrant aromas. As the bees are drawn to the nectar in the flower, if you start putting out the right things, your praise will draw in the Most High God. He doesn't inhabit your fears, your doubts, your complaints, or your worries. Praise is what causes God to work.

I would hear my mother going through the house thanking God for His goodness, talking about how He was turning things around. In the midst of that difficulty, she was singing and making melody in her heart. She could have been making worry, making discouragement, making fear, but she chose to create an atmosphere of praise. She knew that God can smell praise, that He's drawn to praise, so she kept her harp out and kept sending up praises. It didn't happen overnight, but she started getting better and better. That was forty-three years ago, and she's still going strong, healthy and whole. What kind of atmosphere are you creating? What are you sending up all through the day? "I'll never get well. I'll never meet the right person. I can't accomplish my dreams. I don't have the connections." Do yourself a favor and get your harp.

Get your song back. Get your praise back. Get your vision back. Get your dream back. God is still

> *Get your song back. Get your praise back. Get your vision back. Get your dream back.*

on the throne. He still has a destiny for you to fulfill. What's in your future is greater than anything you've seen in the past. You and God are a majority. There's not an obstacle you're facing that He can't turn around. There's not a dream He's put in your heart that He can't bring to pass.

TURN UP THE PRAISE

In 2 Kings 3, the armies of Israel, Judah, and Edom had been traveling together through the desert for seven days. They were going to sneak up and attack the Moabites. They thought there would be streams or wells along the way, but they couldn't find any water and were in serious trouble. They didn't know if they could continue. King Jehoshaphat of Judah asked the other kings if there was any prophet among them who could ask God what they should do. They said that the prophet Elisha was there, but he didn't want to have anything to do with the king of Israel, who didn't honor God. Elisha was annoyed, but because of his friendship with King Jehoshaphat, he agreed to do it anyway. He said, "Bring me someone who can play the harp." Elisha knew he couldn't hear from God when he was irritated and upset. He had to change the atmosphere. The Scripture says, "While the harp was being played, the power of the Lord came on Elisha, and he began to prophesy." It's amazing what God will do if you create the right atmosphere. When there's worry, doubt, and frustration, that keeps us from seeing the goodness of God. Like Elisha did, you have to bring in the harp. Turn up the praise. Create an atmosphere of faith, hope, and expectancy. That's what causes God to show up.

> *This shouldn't be something we do every once in a while. It should be a lifestyle.*

This shouldn't be something we do every once in a while. It should be a lifestyle. David said, "His praise should continually be in our mouth." All through the day, under our breath, we're making melody in our heart. We're thanking God for His goodness, grateful for what He's done, and talking about His greatness. As the bee is attracted to the smell of the flower, God is attracted to the smell of praise. My question is, What kind of atmosphere are you creating? Worry, doubt, and complaining? That's sending out an offensive odor. That's pushing away good things. God is looking for a sweet-smelling aroma. You may be in a difficult situation, things are coming against you, but don't hang up your harp. The enemy would love for you to start complaining and live bitter. No, keep the praises going up. Keep thanking God that He's working. Keep declaring that you're coming out. Keep speaking the blessing. One thing I've learned is that you can't keep a praiser down. If you stay full of praise, I believe and declare that as with Jonah, negative situations are about to turn around and promises will come to pass. You're going to see favor in greater ways, healing, freedom, and divine connections, the fullness of your destiny. It's going to turn out better than you ever imagined.

ACKNOWLEDGMENTS

In this book I offer many stories shared with me by friends, members of our congregation, and people I've met around the world. I appreciate and acknowledge their contributions and support. Some of those mentioned in the book are people I have not met personally, and in a few cases, we've changed the names to protect the privacy of individuals. I give honor to all those to whom honor is due. As the son of a church leader and a pastor myself, I've listened to countless sermons and presentations, so in some cases I can't remember the exact source of a story.

I am indebted to the amazing staff of Lakewood Church, the wonderful members of Lakewood who share their stories with me, and those around the world who generously support our ministry and make it possible to bring hope to a world in need. I am grateful to all those who follow our services on television, the

Internet, SiriusXM, and through the podcasts. You are all part of our Lakewood family.

I offer special thanks also to all the pastors across the country who are members of our Champions Network.

Once again, I am grateful for a wonderful team of professionals who helped me put this book together for you. Leading them is my FaithWords/Hachette publisher, Daisy Hutton, along with Patsy Jones and the team at FaithWords. I truly appreciate the editorial contributions of wordsmith Lance Wubbels, and a special thanks to Phil Munsey for his insights and friendship.

I am grateful also to my literary agents Jan Miller Rich and Shannon Marven at Dupree Miller & Associates.

And last but not least, thanks to my wife, Victoria, and our children, Alexandra and Jonathan and his wife, Sophia, who are my sources of daily inspiration. Thanks as well to our closest family members, who serve as day-to-day leaders of our ministry, including my mother, Dodie; my brother, Paul, and his wife, Jennifer; my sister Lisa and her husband, Kevin; and my brother-in-law Don and his wife, Jackelyn.

We Want to Hear from You!

Each week, I close our international television broadcast by giving the audience an opportunity to make Jesus the Lord of their lives. I'd like to extend that same opportunity to you. Are you at peace with God? A void exists in every person's heart that only God can fill. I'm not talking about joining a church or finding religion. I'm talking about finding life and peace and happiness. Would you pray with me today? Just say, "Lord Jesus, I repent of my sins. I ask You to come into my heart. I make You my Lord and Savior."

Friend, if you prayed that simple prayer, I believe you have been "born again." I encourage you to attend a good Bible-based church and keep God in first place in your life. For free information on how you can grow stronger in your spiritual life, please feel free to contact us.

Victoria and I love you, and we'll be praying for you. We're believing for God's best for you, that you will see your dreams come to pass. We'd love to hear from you!

To contact us, write to:

Joel and Victoria Osteen
PO Box #4271
Houston, TX 77210

Or you can reach us online at joelosteen.com.